To Cindy, Leslie, Nancy, Sonia, and Theo for their patience and good nature as they walked with me over miles of prairie in the heat of the summer.

Note to Readers: Terms defined in glossary are **bold** in the text. In most cases, measurements are given in both metric and English units. Wherever measurements are given in only one system, the units provided are the most appropriate for that situation.

Photographs © 2002: Dembinsky Photo Assoc.: 6 (Willard Clay), 33, 62 (Adam Jones), 102 top (Anthony Mercieca), 52 top, 52 bottom (Rod Planck), 84 (Richard Hamilton Smith); Photo Researchers, NY: 101 (R. Austing), 102 bottom (Bill Dyer), cover (Adam Jones), 34 (Tom & Pat Leeson), 13 (Carolyn A. McKeone); Visuals Unlimited: 102 center (Gary Carter), 13 inset (Tom Uhlman).

Illustrations by Robert Italiano
Book interior design and pagination by Carole Desnoes

Library of Congress Cataloging-in-Publication Data

Martin, Patricia A. Fink, 1955-
    Prairies, fields, and meadows / Patricia A. Fink Martin.
        p. cm. – (Exploring ecosystems)
    Includes bibliographical references (p.).
    ISBN 0-531-11859-2 (lib. bdg.)   0-531-16604-X (pbk.)
        1. Prairie ecology—Juvenile literature. 2. Meadow ecology—Juvenile literature. [1. Prairie ecology. 2. Meadow ecology. 3. Ecology.] I. Title.
II. Series.
QH87.7 .M37 2002
577.4'4—dc21   2001017570

1 2 3 4 5 6 7 8 9 10 R 11 10 09 08 07 06 05 04 03 02

Contents

Introduction

WHERE WOULD YOU GO TO EXPLORE nature and see wildlife in action? A forest, the mountains, the shore? A grassy field might not be first on your list! What could you possibly see standing waist-high in a thick stand of stems and leaves? But imagine if you could shrink yourself and step inside the grassy jungle. Into whose eyes would you be staring as you peered between the tall, green blades?

In this meter-high wilderness, a harvest mouse climbs as nimbly among the grassy stalks as a monkey leaps between the treetops of the rain forest. Continuing on through the grasses, you watch a spider snare its victim in an elaborate web, sink poisonous fangs into the body, and suck out the fluids. Farther ahead, clinging to a stem, a caterpillar twists and turns to escape an attacking wasp. The wasp stabs the caterpillar with the tip of its abdomen, lays a few eggs, and quickly flies away. If you came back in a week or two, you'd see the developing larvae feasting on the caterpillar's body.

A lot goes on down in the grasses! A grassy field is a feast for countless plant-eaters that dine on leaves, stems, seeds, flowers, and roots. Predators stalk the diners from the ground, trap them in silken webs, or dive-bomb them from the air. Bacteria, fungi, and other scavengers feed on the dead or dying. This web of life, shaped by the elements of earth, fire, and weather, is called an **ecosystem**.

Theodore Roosevelt National Park in North Dakota

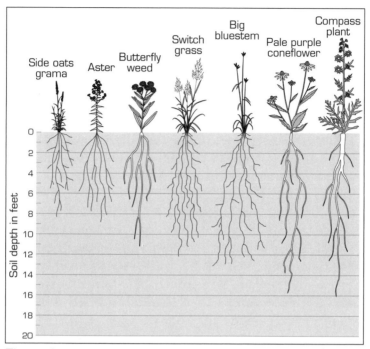

Figure 1 Plant Depth

The field is a grassland ecosystem because it is dominated by grasses.

Grasslands are very different from forests or deserts. You can easily recognize a grassland by its cover of grasses and lack of trees. Wildflowers, called **forbs** by plant scientists, often grow in the midst of the grasses.

Some grasslands carpet plains as flat as tabletops while others swell and dip over rolling hills and ride up steep ridges and on top of bluffs. Because the landscape is open, winds blow unchecked across the land. While more rain falls here than in a desert, a grassland typically receives less rain than a forest. Extended dry periods, or **droughts**, are common. Grassland plants survive by being long-lived and persisting mostly underground. The stems and leaves that you see are only a small part of these plants. Grasses send a thick, tangled mat of roots threading through the soil, some reaching down almost 3 meters (10 ft.). The roots of forbs can plunge even deeper.

Grasslands, by Many Other Names

While scientists use the term grassland to describe these grassy landscapes, they are known by many other names. In South Africa lies the veld, discovered and named by Dutch settlers. The African savanna, a grassland dotted with short, thorny trees and shrubs, sweeps across central Africa. South America boasts several extensive grasslands, from the llanos of Venezuela and Colombia in the north, to the campos of Brazil and the pampas of Argentina in the south. Across northeastern Europe and central Asia spreads the Eurasian steppes. Grasslands also occur in Australia and New Zealand, where they are often called downs.

The North American Prairie

In North America, French trappers discovered the eastern edge of a vast grassland that they named prairie. Sweeping out of central Canada, the prairie ran south for 2,400 kilometers (1,500 mi.) and reached 1,600 kilometers (1,000 mi.) across. Had those trappers traveled westward, they would have seen grasses waist high or taller give way to knee-high grasses, then to grasses only shin high. Today these three regions are known as the **tallgrass prairie, mixed prairie**, and **shortgrass prairie** (see map).

Where can you go to see a tallgrass prairie? Most of the tallgrass prairie has been plowed under, but bits and pieces can still be seen in Illinois, Indiana, Missouri, Iowa, Minnesota, and Nebraska. This prairie supports a thick, lush carpet of grasses and wildflowers. In some places, grasses send flowering stalks as high as 2 to 3 meters (6 to 10 ft.) into the air. Here, a person could get lost among the stems and leaves in this grassy jungle.

If you travel west through much of North and South

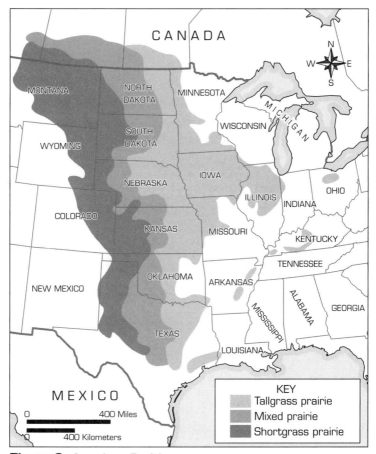

Figure 2 American Prairies

Dakota, Nebraska, Kansas, and Oklahoma, you'll discover the mixed prairie, also called the Great Plains. Shorter grasses and wildflowers make up the landscape. Fewer tall grasses grow on this dry, windy prairie.

Next visit Montana or the eastern parts of Wyoming, Colorado, or New Mexico. You may think you've reached the desert, but you're actually in the shortgrass prairie region or the High Plains. The plains turn green only briefly in the spring. You'll find prickly pear cactus and fringed sagebrush here. Grasses grow sparsely, attaining heights of only 0.5 meter (1.6 ft.).

The North American prairie was once ranked as one of the largest expanses of grassland in the world and is the main subject of this book. Smaller, isolated grasslands lie to the west of the prairie. To the east of the prairie, forests clothe the land, but grassy fields are also common. While most of these are but man-made, temporary landscapes, they often harbor some prairie species.

What Happened to the Trees?

It is forests that the European explorers first encountered in America. As the country grew, settlers began migrating westward, soon reaching the central prairie. The absence of trees astounded them. What happened to the trees? Some felt the soil was too poor to support tree growth. Others thought that strong winds were to blame.

Today scientists point to geologic events that began 65 million years ago in western North America. The earth's crust buckled and heaved upward, forming great mountains and forever altering the weather to the east. As moist air blows in from over the Pacific Ocean, it runs into the mountains and up their slopes. As the air rises, it cools, causing rain or snow to fall. East of the mountains, a **rain shadow** is created because the dry air pushing past the mountains brings with it little rain. In this drier climate, trees lost out to the drought-adapted grasses. Long after the mountains formed, glaciers scoured the central Midwest. Then, about 8,000 years ago, the climate warmed and the glaciers receded. Grasses spread eastward, creating the prairie.

Once the prairie formed, fire and grazing animals helped keep out the trees. Accidental fires started by lightning or Native Americans often blazed across the prairie. Tree seedlings and shrubs burned, while grasses sent up new shoots within days of the disaster. **Bison** and pronghorn tore at and chomped on young shoots and buds, destroying tree saplings and shrubs. But, unlike trees and shrubs that grow from buds at the tips of branches, grasses sprout from their base. Their leaves can be chewed, clipped, trampled, or even burned, but the grasses keep on growing.

Creatures of the Grasses

The prairie is an ecosystem subject to extremes. Fire is not the only disturbance common to the prairie. High winds, thunderstorms, tornadoes, drought, frigid cold, and searing heat often visit the prairie. What animals can live in such a place?

The early prairie explorers and settlers found huge herds of bison, elk, and pronghorn. Much to their surprise, they also found lots of holes and tunnels in the ground! Many prairie animals live in the soil. Pocket gophers, prairie dogs, deer mice, jumping mice, and several kinds of ground squirrels dig burrows to escape heat, cold, fire, and predators.

Wolves, coyotes, and grizzly bears hunted the large grazers of the prairie, while foxes, badgers, ferrets, and hawks pursued the smaller game. In the spring millions of birds migrated to the prairie to breed. Insects chewed, clipped, and tore at green leaves, **pollinated** flowers, and drank nectar, while birds, spiders, and small mammals plucked the insects out of the grasses for a bite to eat.

Today, the wild, native prairie has shrunk in size, but if you search hard, you can still find places where bison graze, prairie dogs pop in and out of their burrows, and badgers hunt them down. The prairie still hums with the sounds of grasshoppers and rings with the cries of feathered migrants. Hordes of plant-eaters continue to feast on the bounty of leaves, stems, seeds, flowers, and roots.

An Invitation to Explore

You don't have to travel to Africa for an exciting grassland adventure. Plan a safari to a prairie, meadow, or grassy field. Use the activities described in this book to explore these special places. Go on an egg hunt—for butterfly eggs the size of pinheads! Learn how to make food from grasses. Sharpen your sleuthing skills as you search for secretive grassland mammals. Plan a stake-out outside a burrow. Become a grassland explorer. Many new and exciting discoveries await you!

Safety First and Last

While a grassland is a relatively tame wilderness to explore, play it safe. Keep the following guidelines in mind.

- Wear hiking boots or sturdy walking shoes. Watch out for burrow openings (holes) in the ground.
- Be on the lookout for plants with sharp spines and thorns, poison ivy, and other offensive plants.
- Learn to recognize poison ivy and stinging nettle. Stinging nettle's entire surface is covered with tiny hairs that will sting you if you brush up against them. Poison ivy's pollen and resin on the leaves and stems can easily irritate exposed skin.
- Find out if hunting is allowed in the area you'll be exploring. Plan your trips during times when few hunters will be out.
- Protect yourself from mosquitoes, ticks, and chiggers. Wear long pants and socks. Use insect repellent on your legs, especially around the ankles. Stick to the walking trails. Search yourself for ticks when you get home. If a rash develops near a tick bite, see a doctor immediately.
- Learn to recognize the poisonous snakes that inhabit the area you'll be exploring. Listen for the warning rattle of a rattlesnake. Carry a hiking stick to probe the grasses ahead of you.
- Wear a hat and use sunscreen to protect your skin. Bring along plenty of drinking water to keep cool.
- Keep an eye to the sky to watch for approaching storms. Thunderstorms and windstorms can develop suddenly.

*Stinging nettle is covered with tiny hairs that will sting you if you
brush up against them.*

Keeping A Journal

Keeping a record of your experiences is easy and can be quite rewarding. All you need is a bound notebook and a pen with waterproof ink or a pencil. Choose a notebook large enough to allow for sketches and notes, but small enough to easily fit inside a backpack. Protect your notebook by keeping it in a large reclosable bag, or better yet, purchase a notebook made of water-resistant paper (see Appendix for a list of suppliers).

As you explore grasslands, keep your journal with you. Write down your observations and any questions that come to you while you're out in the field. Don't think you can remember everything until you get back home! It's easy to forget the details, so write them down while they're fresh in your mind. Even if you're not an artist, include sketches of what you see.

CHAPTER 1

Plants of The Grasslands

TO SOME EARLY EUROPEAN EXPLORERS, the prairie, with its waves of wind-tossed leaves spreading as far as the horizon, was a sea of grass. To others, the prairie was a beautiful meadow of wildflowers. To all, it was a mostly treeless landscape.

In terms of the number of leaves and stems, the grasses win the count. The prairie truly is a grassland. Even though grasses once covered half our country, few Americans can name one native prairie grass. Can you? Do names like big bluestem, little bluestem, Indian grass, sand dropseed, or switch grass sound familiar? Probably not!

Still, most of us can recognize a grass plant. But what is a grass? Grasses are low-growing, non-woody or **herbaceous** plants. Their round, sometimes flattened, hollow stems are marked with solid joints or **nodes**. Nodes are places where the leaves attach. Each leaf consists of two parts—a narrow **blade** and a section that encircles the stem. While grasses do

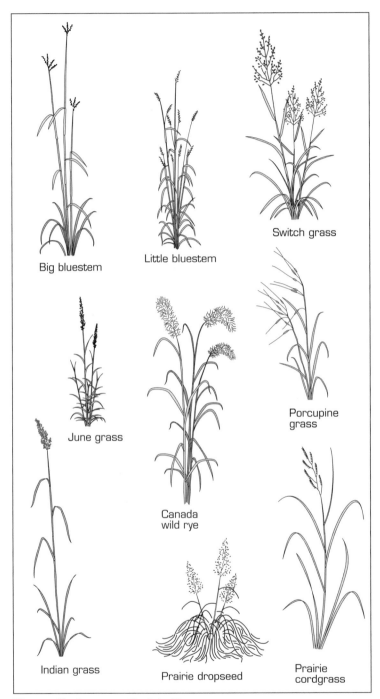

Figure 3 Common Prairie Grasses

flower, their flowers are quite small and easily over-looked.

Some grasses grow best in the cooler weather of spring and fall. These cool-season grasses green up and flower early in the year. They slow their growth in the hot, summer months but may have a second growth period in the fall. Warm-season grasses renew their growth much later in the spring. They thrive during the hot weather of summer.

Grasses can also be categorized by the way they grow. Prairie grasses, such as little bluestem or blue grama, grow in large clumps or bunches. They are called bunch-grasses. You may count well over 100 stems in a single clump. Other prairie grasses, such as Indian grass and big bluestem, form a thick mat of stems and leaves that completely covers the ground. Their fibrous roots penetrate every centimeter of topsoil, binding the soil so firmly that settlers often built their houses with blocks of the **sod**.

Grasses aren't the only plants on the prairie. Showy wildflowers or forbs grow amidst the grasses. Many of the forbs belong to two major plant families: the daisy family and the pea or bean family.

Prairie forbs flower from early spring to late fall, with three major peaks of flowering. But, if you wanted to catch them all, you must visit a site almost daily. Early in the spring, a small group of forbs show their blossoms. Most of these early forbs, like the pasque flower, grow close to the ground. Summer is decorated with a glorious parade of color as violets, irises, orchids, clovers, and others reveal their blooms. The flowering season ends with a final spurt of blossoms in early fall, when goldenrod and asters add a sprinkling of gold and white to the scene.

Use the activities that follow to learn more about prairie wildflowers and the often-ignored prairie grasses.

Figure 4 Prairie Wildflowers by Month

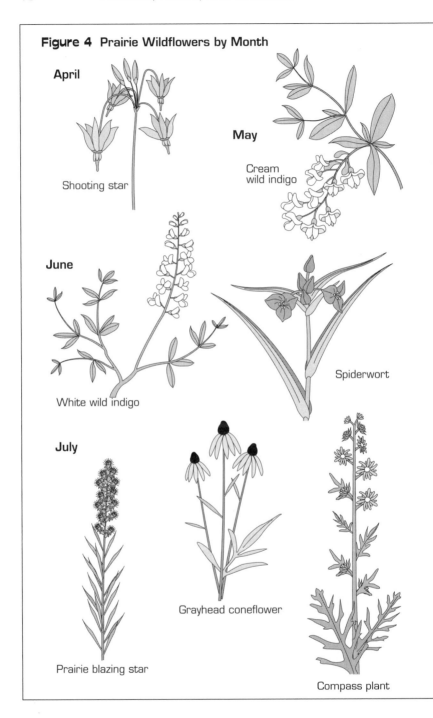

April

Shooting star

May

Cream
wild indigo

June

White wild indigo

Spiderwort

July

Grayhead coneflower

Prairie blazing star

Compass plant

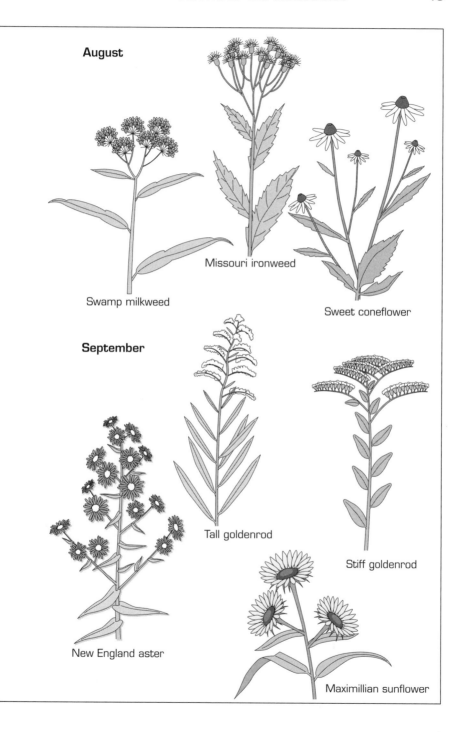

August

Missouri ironweed

Swamp milkweed

Sweet coneflower

September

Tall goldenrod

Stiff goldenrod

New England aster

Maximillian sunflower

Introduction to Wildflowers

In nature we are drawn to colorful things—birds, butterflies, autumn leaves, and wildflowers. Wildflowers are especially popular and they are well represented on the prairie. Unlike birds and butterflies, they won't fly away just when you have them in your sights!

Getting to know wildflowers doesn't take a lot of equipment. You'll need a hand lens, tweezers, single-edged razor blade, flowers (gladioluses or lilies work well) from a florist's shop, a field guide to wildflowers, and your journal.

Wildflowers are often identified by the color and structure of their flowers. While there may seem to be an infinite variety in the colors and shapes of wildflowers, most flowers have the same basic parts. Learning these parts will help you in identifying wildflowers in the field.

Pluck one flower from a stem. Look at it carefully. The outermost circle of flower parts, the **calyx**, consists of several, small, green leaves called **sepals**. (In some flowers, these may be colored). Pull these off your flower. You can't miss the showy **petals** just inside the sepals. Together the petals make up the **corolla**. How many petals does your flower have? Pull the petals apart to reveal several, long, thin stalks, each supporting an enlarged, colored tip. These are the male parts of the flower. They are called **stamens**. Each stamen is made up of a long, thin filament that supports an **anther**. Break open an anther to observe the powdery **pollen** inside.

The innermost or female part of the flower is called the **pistil**. It is made up of three main structures: the **ovary**, the **style**, and the **stigma**. Follow the thin, white stalk or style to the base of the flower. Here you will find the bulb-like ovary. Use a single-edged razor blade to cut a cross section. With a hand lens, you should be able to see small chambers, each containing a round **ovule**. Now examine the tip of the style, where you'll see the stigma. It may be branched. Take a closer look with your hand lens. You'll see tiny hairs that help trap the pollen released by the anthers.

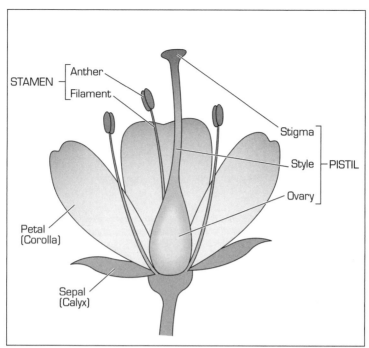

Figure 5 Diagram of a Flower

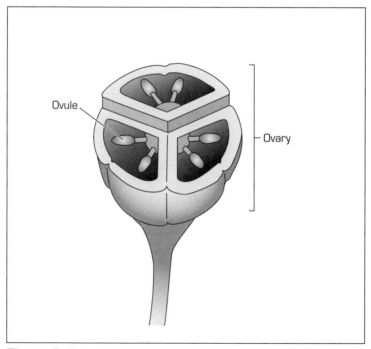

Figure 6 Cross Section of an Ovary

Knowing the basic parts of a flower will help you learn the names of the wildflowers that you find outdoors. Note the color and shape of the petals and sepals, as well as the number and arrangement of pistil, stamens, petals, and sepals. Keep an eye out for wildflowers along roadsides and railroad tracks, and in fields, meadows, prairies, woodlands, pastures, and empty lots. Don't pick the flowers! Use a camera to capture the image and leave the flowers themselves for others to enjoy.

Wildflowers of the Grassland: Spotlight on the Daisy[1] Family

While prairies may be grasslands in terms of the number of leaves and stems, three out of four prairie plants are wildflowers. One group, the daisy family, is especially common on the prairie. Becoming familiar with this plant group will give you a good start towards identifying the wildflowers that you find in your explorations.

Gather a hand lens, tweezers, field guide to wildflowers, and your journal. Visit a florist to pick up some daisies.

Select one daisy from the bunch. Although it looks like a single flower, you are actually looking at over a hundred tiny flowers. Two types of small flowers, **disk flowers** and **ray flowers**, make up the flower head of the daisy. Disk flowers compose the central eye of the daisy, while ray flowers make up the outer white ring.

Use your fingers to gently open up the daisy. Pull it apart from the sides, then separate the parts with tweezers. Can you distinguish a ray flower from a disk flower? View each with a hand lens. In the disk flower, you'll notice that the petals of the corolla fuse to form a tube. Protruding from the opening

---

[1] This family is also known as the sunflower or aster family. The scientific family name is Asteraceae or Compositae.

of the tube you should see the style and stigma. The anthers are pressed up against the style. Now examine a ray flower. In some members of the daisy family, the corolla of a ray flower consists of a single, petal-like blade. You should also be able to locate the style, stigma, and anthers in these flowers. How many ray flowers and disk flowers make up a daisy?

Next stroll through a nearby field or empty lot. Look for dandelions, black-eyed Susans, goldenrods, sunflowers, asters, and other daisy-like flowers using your field guide. Examine the flowers with a hand lens. You'll find that not all flowers in this plant family consist of both ray and disk flowers. In some, the flower head consists of one type or the other, but not both.

✔ Doing More
Take a wildflower tour of select prairies across the United States, online. Look at wildflowers of Kansas prairies at

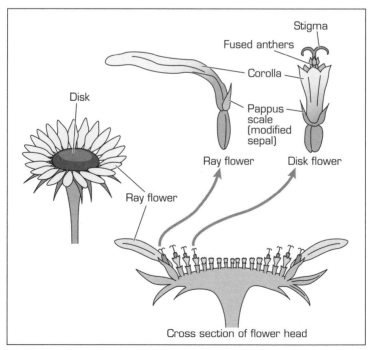

Figure 7 Flower Head of Composites (Daisy Family)

http://spuds.agron.ksu.edu/wildflw.htm. Hook up to Meadowbrook's Web site at http://www.prairienet.org/meadow brook/year.html. View a catalog of tallgrass prairie wildflowers at http://www.inhs.uiuc.edu/~kenr/prairieplants.

Visit a local greenhouse to closely observe the plant parts of different kinds of plants.

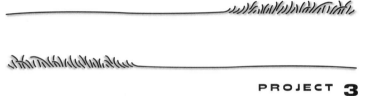

PROJECT **3**

Secret Wildflowers: The Anatomy of a Grass Plant

When you were younger, did you ever chase your friends with mock whips of grass blades or tickle them with a grass's feather-like head? Now that you're older, take a second look at that plant that you ripped apart so easily as a child! There's much more to a grass plant than meets the eye.

To study the parts of a grass up close, you'll need a hand lens or dissecting microscope (borrow one from your school science lab), a long-shafted screwdriver, single-edged razor blades, plastic garbage bags with twist ties, fine-tipped tweezers, paper towels, and your journal.

Grasses may be as close as your front lawn, but search a little farther afield. From early spring to late fall, you'll find grasses growing along roadsides and railroad tracks, and in prairies, fields, pastures, and empty lots. Avoid grassy plants growing in wet areas. Look for plants with jointed stems, long, tapering leaves, and tufts or feathery plumes at the tips of the stems.

To collect a grass plant, loosen the dirt at the plant's base with the shaft of a screwdriver. After working the roots loose, gently pull the plant out of the ground. Store your specimen in a sealed garbage bag. Gather at least five different grasses.

At home or back at school, spread your specimens on a table with good overhead lighting. Not all of the plants that you

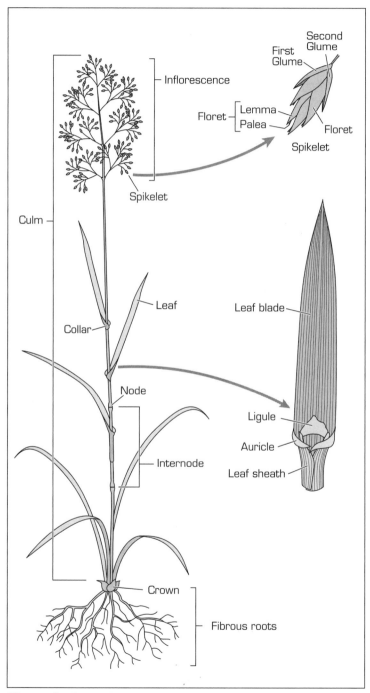

Figure 8 Grass Plant and Spikelet

collected may be grasses. Some could be **rushes** or **sedges**, plant groups that closely resemble the grass family. Study the chart on the next page. Re-examine your specimens and toss out any plants that may be sedges or rushes.

Wash the dirt off the roots of each grass plant. Blot the roots dry. Can you distinguish stems, leaves, and roots? The roots resemble thin strands or fibers of string. Because of their appearance, they are called fibrous roots. You probably left most of the roots of your specimen in the soil when you dug it up. You may also see thick, white, stem-like structures called **rhizomes**. These underground stems often sprout new shoots and roots.

Work your way up the plant to the stems and leaves. Pull a leaf away from the stem. Notice how the leaf wraps around the stem for some distance before sending out a strap-like blade. The part of the leaf wrapped around the stem is called the **sheath**. Examine the inner junction of the blade and sheath, where you may see the **ligule**. The ligule looks like a small flap or a cluster of hairs.

Now turn to the feathery plumes or tufts at the tip of the stem. Can you guess what these are? These tufts consist of clusters of tiny flowers. Although they may not look it, grasses are actually wildflowers. The clusters of tiny flowers are called **spikelets**. They look like groupings of small, immature seeds. Spikelets may be tightly packed along a short stem or spaced far apart on several branches.

Break off a spikelet. Remove the bottom two scales at its base with fine-tipped tweezers. These scales, or **glumes**, look like tiny, empty boats. The rest of the spikelet is composed of two or more tiny flowering units called **florets**. Dissect a floret to reveal an inner and outer scale. The outer scale may be keeled and bear a long bristle or **awn**. When a floret blossoms, two additional structures may appear. With your hand lens, look for small, dangling pods (the anthers) and dark, miniature brushes (the stigma).

PROJECT **4**

Making a Grass Collection

See how many kinds of grasses you can find as you walk through a grassy field. Collect a few flower stalks from each grass. At home, set them upright in a large vase or basket. This will make an attractive dried arrangement, but for a permanent collection, you'll need to press and mount the plants.

Gather a hand lens, long-shafted screwdriver, plastic garbage bags with twist ties, single-edged razor blade, fine-pointed tweezers, tape measure, paper tags, plant press, small index cards, white glue, sponge, cookie sheet, wax paper, mounting paper, and your journal. Professional herbarium mounting paper can be purchased from suppliers or cut to size 29 × 42 centimeters (11.4 × 16.5 in.) from cardstock. Make your own plant press using the directions provided in the Appendix.

As a beginner, limit your collecting to a nearby meadow, field, empty lot, or the county in which you live. If you collect at least bimonthly during the growing season, you'll get a good feel for the parade of grasses that share the land during a year.

Collect grass specimens using the procedures described in Project 3. Select plants with healthy, green leaves and developed flower heads. Before you dig, take a minute to record some critical features that may not be retained in a pressed specimen. Use the checklist on the next page to guide you.

Once you've completed the checklist and dug up the plant, place a paper tag around it and number the tag. Record the tag number in your journal and on the check sheet. Carefully put the plant in a collecting bag, then close it tightly with a twist tie. When you are finished collecting for the day, store your specimens in the refrigerator until you are ready to press them.

To press the plants, first rinse them to remove dirt and insects. Blot the plants dry with paper towels. Be sure to keep the paper tag with each specimen. Now follow the directions given in the Appendix for pressing and mounting.

Table 1 Checklist for Identification of Grasses

Growth Pattern

- ☐ Cool-season grass
- ☐ Warm-season grass
- ☐ Annual
- Perennial
  - ☐ With rhizomes
  - ☐ Without rhizomes

Culms (Stems)

Height (average)
- ☐ ≤ 1/2 meter
- ☐ 1/2 to 1 meter
- ☐ ≥ 1 meter

Width
- ☐ slender
- ☐ robust

Nodes
- ☐ smooth
- ☐ hairy

Leaves

Shape of blade (cross section)
- ☐ flat
- ☐ folded
- ☐ edges rolled

Width of blade
- ☐ ≤ centimeter
- ☐ 1 to 2 centimeter
- ☐ ≥ 2 centimeters

Margin of blade
- ☐ smooth
- ☐ serrated

Surface of blade
- ☐ smooth
- ☐ serrated

Junction of blade and sheath
- ☐ hairy ligule
- ☐ membranous ligule
- ☐ small prongs at lower edge of blade (auricles)

Flower Head

Position on stem
- ☐ terminal
- ☐ lateral

Form
- ☐ Spikelets attached directly to main axis (spike)
- ☐ Spikelets attached to short branch off main axis (raceme)
- ☐ Spikelets attached to multiple branches (panicle)

Spikelet

Shape
- ☐ flattened
- ☐ rounded

Attachment to stem
- ☐ direct
- ☐ via short stalk

Number of florets
- ☐ 1 to 3
- ☐ 4 to 10
- ☐ > 10

Awns
- ☐ present
- ☐ absent

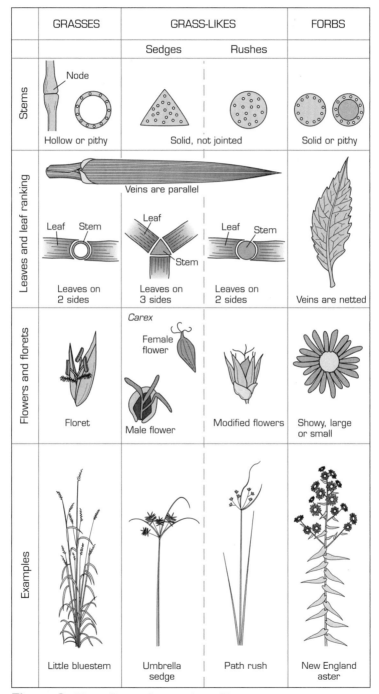

Figure 9 Plant Group Comparison Chart

How will you identify your specimens? While field guides to wildflowers and trees can readily be found, few easy-to-use guides exist for grasses. Try to locate one of those listed in the Appendix. As you thumb through the guide, refer to the mounted specimen, checklist, and any notes or sketches that you made. If you still can't identify the grass, consult a botanist at the nearest university, botanical garden, nature museum, or agricultural extension service. You may be able to mail your specimen to them for identification.

Food from a Grass: Making Flour from Grains of Wheat

A drive through prairie country today will probably take you by more corn and wheat fields than native prairie. Corn and wheat belong to a special group of grasses called grains. Rye, barley, rice, and oats are also grains. The seeds of these six grasses feed most of the world's human population as well as its domestic animals.

With a few, simple pieces of equipment, you can make food from a grass. Borrow a mortar and pestle from your school chemistry lab or a local pharmacist. Wash and dry the mortar and pestle thoroughly before you use it. Visit a natural foods market or health food store to purchase wheat grains, also called wheat berries. You'll also need a cutting board, hand lens or dissecting microscope, single-edged razor blade, flour sifter, a spoon or measuring cup, and a cake pan.

First examine the wheat grain under magnification. Cut a few grains in half using a razor blade. What do you see? The grain of wheat is a seed: a packet of stored food, the **endosperm**, accompanying a tiny plant **embryo** and surrounded by a protective covering called the **bran**. Most of what you'll see in your cut sections is endosperm. Endosperm is used to make the white flour that you buy at the grocery store.

To make wheat flour, scoop a tablespoon of grains into the bowl of the mortar. Pound, grind, scrape, and mash the grains with the pestle. To keep the grains from flying out, cover the mortar with one hand.

After several minutes, you should see a light-colored powder accumulating at the bottom of the mortar. This is flour. But don't stop now! Keep grinding until you've broken most of the kernels. Pour the contents of the mortar into a flour sifter. Holding the cake pan underneath the sifter, sift the flour, then measure it. How much flour did you make? It takes a little over 2 cups of flour to make a loaf of bread. Do you think you can do it? Give it a try! Follow the directions in a general cookbook to bake a loaf of bread from your freshly milled flour.

✔ Doing More

Visit an operating gristmill to learn about the milling process used in America's pioneer days. Collect a few stalks of ripened wheat from a wheat field. Can you dissect the seed heads and thresh out the grains?

CHAPTER **2**

Exploring Grassy Landscapes

GAZING OUT AT A PRAIRIE AS YOU course along a highway, you may only catch a blur of tans and greens brightened with an occasional spot of orange, yellow, or white. Even to many of the early pioneers, traveling at a wagon's pace, the prairie was but a blur, a seemingly endless carpet of grass.

Simple as it may look, the prairie is not a monotonous cover of similar grasses and forbs. In some areas, more than 300 plant species crowd onto an acre of prairie, yet in other parts of the prairie, you may see fewer than ten species.

As the prairie sweeps across the land, it encounters changing weather patterns and soil types. Some plant species become less abundant or disappear altogether. New species, better adapted to the changing conditions, appear on the scene.

Even within a single prairie region, soils and parent rock types can differ. The tallgrass prairie is especially diverse. Scientists often recognize the following natural prairie communities within the tallgrass region: black soil prairie, sand prairie, gravel prairie, dolomite prairie, and hill prairie. Each supports a slightly different but overlapping constellation of plant species.

Different soil moisture levels also create variety within the tallgrass prairie. Here a prairie visitor might see wet patches, moist soils, and even dry areas. Because different plants grow in these areas, scientists distinguish them as wet prairie, mesic prairie, and dry prairie. Dry

Mesic prairies grow the greatest variety of wildflowers because the soil is moist through most of the growing season.

The prairie dog contributes to the diversity of the prairies.

prairies often occur on hilltops or ridges that are well drained. Mesic prairies look quite lush. This prairie type grows the greatest variety of wildflowers of any of the prairies. Moisture is present in the soil through most of the growing season. On a wet prairie, wear boots when you visit, for the soil will be mucky and muddy, especially in the spring.

Through their daily activities, animals too contribute to prairie diversity. Creatures from insects, like grasshoppers and ants, to larger animals, like the bison, all change the prairie in some way. Ant hills, prairie dog mounds, buffalo wallows, deer bedding sites, well-traveled animal trails, and single hoof prints all represent altered sites or microhabitats. Even a spot where an animal urinates or defecates represents a change in the environment. Only certain plant species favor these disturbed sites. Because these areas differ from their surroundings, they are called patches. A patch can be as small as an individual plant or a shady spot under a ledge or as large as a cluster of shrubs or a colony of forbs several meters in diameter.

Use the activities of this chapter to explore the diversity of a prairie and other special grasslands. You'll never again view a grassland as a monotonous ocean of grass!

A First Look at a Grassland: Mapping the Landscape

What does every explorer need when exploring a new land? A map, of course! To make an accurate map of part of a grassland, you'll need a hammer, 14 stakes, 120 meters (400 ft.) of lightweight cord or rope, a 30-meter (100-ft.) measuring tape, surveyor's flagging or strips of fabric, a permanent marker, and your journal. ***Beware of chiggers, ticks, holes in the ground, and too much sun! Review the safety rules given in the Introduction.***

Measure 60 meters (200 ft.) along one edge of a grassland you wish to investigate. Hammer a stake into the ground at each end of the stretch. Tie a cord from stake to stake to establish a baseline. Along this baseline, use flagging to mark five stations at 10-meter (33-ft.) intervals. Number the stations consecutively with a marker.

Run a line or **transect** from Station 1, 60 meters (200 ft.) out across the field. The transect should be **perpendicular** to the baseline. To estimate a perpendicular line, stand at the station facing the grassland. Hold your arms straight out to the sides, palms facing forward. Your arms should be **parallel** to the baseline. Now close your eyes and, with your fingers outstretched, bring your arms together in front of you until your palms touch. Open your eyes and sight an imaginary line along your arms and fingers to a spot about 60 meters (200 ft.) away. That line will be perpendicular to the baseline.

Set the transect by placing a stake in the ground to mark the spot. Stretch a cord from Station 1 to that stake. Using the measuring tape, determine the distance from the station to any features you wish to include on your map—a clump of shrubs, a tree, the bank of a stream or small pond, a small hill or mound, or the burrow of some ground-dweller. Record the distances in your journal. Continue mapping by running transects across the prairie from all stations and taking measurements at each station.

When you have completed the measurements, you are ready to draw your map. It's easiest to work at home on a table or desk. You'll need paper, a protractor, a ruler, and a pencil.

First, choose a map scale. Maps are representations of real-life settings drawn on a smaller scale so that all the information fits on one page. Try letting 1 centimeter on the map equal 5 meters (1 in. = 40 ft.) in real measurement.

Now draw the baseline to scale. Mark and label the stations. Draw the transects using a protractor to ensure they are perpendicular to the baseline. Using the information that you collected in the field, mark the distances to key landmarks you wish to include on your map.

✔ Doing More

Take another sojourn through the prairie. This time around, document the plant species that live there. Walk each transect line slowly. Don't try to identify every grass, forb, or shrub that you come across. It's easier to focus on one plant form at a time. For example, first look at wildflowers. Identify any wildflowers you don't know using a field guide. Keep a list in your journal.

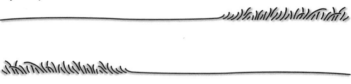

A Mosaic of Plants: Looking at Plant Distribution Patterns in a Grassland

By now, you've probably noticed that the prairie is not quite as uniform as it appears. But why not? To answer this question, plant ecologists look to environmental factors, such as soil moisture, **pH**, or nitrogen. Sometimes such factors change gradually across an area. These small, incremental changes make up a **gradient**. Because some plants have distinct preferences for certain levels of these factors, they will arrange themselves in a definite pattern along a gradient—each growing only in a narrow band.

Challenge yourself to find an environmental gradient on a nearby prairie or other grassland. Profile the plants along the gradient to illustrate the changes in the plant community. You'll need a 7-meter (25-ft.) measuring tape, a ruler, 30 meters (100 ft.) of lightweight rope, several stakes, surveyor's flagging or strips of brightly colored fabric, field guides to grasses and wildflowers, your journal, a hand calculator, and copies of the data sheets included in this activity. The best time to do this activity is the late spring or early summer during the peak growing season. *Think safety! Review the safety rules for exploring grasslands given in the Introduction.*

Once you've found a grassy field or prairie, take a minute to stroll through it. Look for low spots and high areas or a slope in the land. Changes in the topography may result in a soil moisture gradient, as water drains off upland slopes and is retained in low areas. Examine the ground—do you see areas of standing water or places where the soil is dry and cracked?

When you've located a potential gradient, place a stake at each extreme. Run a line between the stakes. This line is called a transect. Mark off equally spaced intervals along the transect line with flagging or fabric strip. Select interval spacings of 2 to 5 meters (6 to 16 ft.).

Walk to one end of the transect. Decide on one plant form (grasses, forbs, or shrubs) to survey first. Next, identify each plant of that type, whose leaves, stems, or flowers touch, lie directly below, directly above, or within a hand's width of the transect line. Record the name of each species and number of plants on the data sheet (Table 2). Because individual grass plants are hard to distinguish, count separate clumps as individuals. When you reach the first flag along the transect, continue your survey but record the data on a second data sheet, labeling it Transect 1, Interval 2. Each

Table 2 Plant Sampling Data Sheet
Line-Intercept Method

Date: _____

Habitat: _____

Location: _____

Plant form surveyed (circle one):

      Grasses   Forbs (Wildflowers)   Shrubs

Interval number: _____

Plant Number	Plant Species

Table 3 Summary Data Sheet from Line-Intercept Plant Survey

Date: _____

Habitat: _____

Location: _____

Plant form surveyed (circle one):

Grasses   Forbs (Wildflowers)   Shrubs

Plant Species	Intercept Interval—Number of Individuals						Total for Species
	1	2	3	4	5	6	

time you begin surveying a new section, start a new data sheet.

Analyze your data using the Summary Data Sheet (Table 3). First list each species that you recorded along the transect. Next, record the number of individual plants of that species found in each consecutive interval. In the totals column, add the total number of individuals counted for each species.

Which species are abundant? Which plants are sparse? Do you notice any species whose distribution is skewed towards one end or the other of the transect? Which plants appear to be evenly distributed down the transect line?

✔ Doing More

Soil moisture is just one environmental factor that affects the distribution of plant species. Can you think of other factors that might influence how plants are arranged in a landscape?

PROJECT **8**

Tracking the Seasons: Keeping a Grassland Journal

In the forests of America's national parks, the appearance of the first spring flowers attracts visitors from near and far. Yet, the seasonal parade of color on a prairie can be just as spectacular and last much longer. From spring through fall, prairie visitors view a kaleidoscope of colors as wildflowers of many kinds come into bloom. At the peak of flowering, each day brings the fresh blossoms of yet a different species.

Next spring, keep a diary of the seasonal changes in a nearby prairie or grassy field. You'll need a notebook or your journal, a pencil or pen, graph paper, a field guide to wildflowers, a 30-meter (100-ft.) measuring tape, stakes or poles about 1 meter (3 ft.) in length, a hammer, and surveyor's flagging or strips of brightly colored fabric. A camera and film would also come in handy. *Wear long pants and thick socks to protect against chiggers and ticks!*

Once you've collected these items, choose a grassland close to home to study. Obtain permission from the land-owner to study the field. In late winter, visit the site with stakes, a hammer, flagging or fabric strips, and a tape mea-sure. Place four stakes in the ground along one edge of the area, about 5 meters (16 ft.) apart. Tie flagging or fabric strips around the tops of the poles to make them more visi-ble. Now stand in front of the first stake and walk 25 meters (80 ft.) out into the grasses. Mark the distance with a stake and flagging. Repeat the procedure for each of the other three stakes. These poles will mark study paths along which you will travel to make your observations.

Begin making observations in late winter. Visit your study site twice a week until the first sign of plant growth. At that time, start visiting the site daily. At each visit, record weather conditions, the date, and the time of day. Walk along each marked path, peering carefully into the dried stalks. The ear-liest wildflowers often go unnoticed because they are small and grow close to the ground. In addition to identifying the plants in bloom, record the number of blossoms. At the end of each visit, tally the number of blooms for each plant species in flower. Continue making daily visits through spring, sum-

Figure 10 Flowering Chart

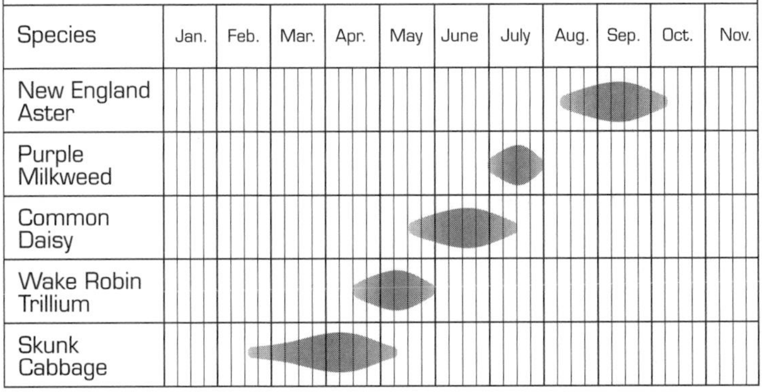

Species	Jan.	Feb.	Mar.	Apr.	May	June	July	Aug.	Sep.	Oct.	Nov.
New England Aster											
Purple Milkweed											
Common Daisy											
Wake Robin Trillium											
Skunk Cabbage											

mer, and fall, until the first frost or the last of the wildflowers makes its appearance.

Graph your observations using the format shown in the figure on the next page. To fit all your data on one graph, tape several sheets of graph paper together. Chart the date of first flowering, maximum flowering, and last flowering for each species.

✔ Doing More

As you track the flowering of forbs through the growing season, compare the heights of early bloomers and late bloomers. How different are they? Can you explain the difference?

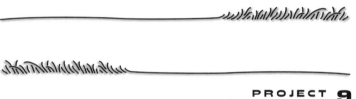

Exploring Special Places I: The North American Prairie

Where would you go to see incredible herds of wildlife galloping across a grassy plain? Africa? One hundred and fifty years ago, you wouldn't have had to leave the country. America's central grassland boasted an amazing abundance of creatures. Where are they now? The North American prairie has given way to farms, ranches, cities, and towns. Today, only fragments remain. Yet, on these isolated patches, you can still see the prairie landscape with many of its original plants and animals.

Plan a prairie expedition. You'll need binoculars, a hand lens, a copy of the checklist on the next page (Table 4), your journal, and a field guide to grasslands (see Appendix for reference). *While a prairie seems like a relatively safe place to explore, play it safe! Read over the safety precautions listed in the Introduction. Pack some drinking water, food, and a first aid kit too.*

Where should you go? If you live in the central United

Table 4 Checklist for Common Plants, Birds, and Mammals of the North American Prairie (including the plains)

Plants

- [ ] Big bluestem
- [ ] Little bluestem
- [ ] Indiangrass
- [ ] Switchgrass
- [ ] Prairie dropseed
- [ ] Prairie cordgrass
- [ ] Junegrass
- [ ] Western wheatgrass
- [ ] Hairy grama
- [ ] Needlegrass
- [ ] Needle-and-thread
- [ ] Buffalo grass
- [ ] Blue grama
- [ ] Prairie dock
- [ ] Rattlesnake master
- [ ] Culver's root
- [ ] Prairie coneflower
- [ ] Compass plant
- [ ] Leadplant
- [ ] Blazing star
- [ ] Tall coreopsis
- [ ] Prairie cinquefoil
- [ ] Common milkweed
- [ ] Butterfly weed
- [ ] Evening primrose
- [ ] Prairie smoke
- [ ] Rough blazing star
- [ ] Indian blanket
- [ ] Poppy mallow
- [ ] Many-spined Opuntia
- [ ] Plains larkspur
- [ ] Common sunflower
- [ ] Pasque flower
- [ ] Mule's ear
- [ ] Plains prickly pear cactus
- [ ] Red false mallow
- [ ] Plains yucca
- [ ] Purple prairie clover
- [ ] Purple locoweed
- [ ] Sand sagebrush
- [ ] Fringed sagebrush

Birds

- [ ] Eastern meadowlark
- [ ] Western meadowlark
- [ ] Dickcissel
- [ ] Bobolink
- [ ] Western kingbird
- [ ] Lark sparrow
- [ ] Grasshopper sparrow
- [ ] Vesper sparrow
- [ ] Upland sandpiper
- [ ] Greater prairie chicken
- [ ] Lesser prairie chicken
- [ ] Sage grouse
- [ ] Magpie
- [ ] Horned lark
- [ ] Killdeer
- [ ] Burrowing owl
- [ ] Swainson's hawk
- [ ] American kestrel
- [ ] Northern harrier
- [ ] Golden eagle

Mammals

- [ ] Badger
- [ ] Franklin's ground squirrel
- [ ] Richardson's ground squirrel
- [ ] 13-lined ground squirrel
- [ ] Ord's kangaroo rat
- [ ] Black-tailed jack rabbit
- [ ] White-tailed jack rabbit
- [ ] Swift fox
- [ ] Kit fox
- [ ] Cottontail rabbit
- [ ] Coyote
- [ ] White-tailed deer
- [ ] Black-tailed deer
- [ ] Black-tailed prairie dog
- [ ] White-tailed prairie dog
- [ ] Elk
- [ ] Mule deer
- [ ] Bison
- [ ] Pronghorn antelope

Table 5   Prairie Parks and Preserves

Tallgrass Prairie

Tallgrass Prairie Preserve, Pawhuska, OK
Konza Prairie, Manhattan, KS
University of Wisconsin-Madison Arboretum, Madison, WI
Tallgrass Prairie National Preserve, Strong City, KS
Prairie State Park, Barton County, MO
Chiwaukee Prairie, WI (on Lake Michigan south of Kenosha)

Mixed Prairie

Wichita Mountains National Wildlife Refuge, Indiahoma, OK
Fort Niobrara National Wildlife Refuge, Valentine, NE
Little Bighorn National Monument, Crow Agency, MT
Wind Cave National Park, Hot Springs, SD
Theodore Roosevelt National Park, Medora, ND

Shortgrass Prairie

Wind Cave National Park, Hot Springs, SD
Buffalo Gap National Wildlife Refuge, Umbarger, TX
Pawnee National Grassland, Greeley, CO
Central Plains Experimental Range, Fort Collins, CO

States or central Canada, you're probably not too far from a prairie preserve. If you live elsewhere, consider stopping in prairie country on your next family vacation. A few prairie preserves are listed above (Table 5). To find others, check the map in the Introduction. Choose a state within the prairie region. Next, contact that state's Department of Natural Resources (use the World Wide Web) to find out about state-managed prairies. The Nature Conservancy, a private organization devoted to protecting the environment, also owns prairie holdings across the prairie region. Check their Web site for locations (see Appendix).

Once you're at a prairie, what should you look for? Each prairie region supports a unique mix of grasses, forbs, and wildlife. Use the checklists and descriptions on the previous page to guide you as you explore.

In the tallgrass prairie, listen for the sounds of meadowlarks and dickcissels. If you like wildflowers, this is the place to be, but don't overlook the grasses. Be sure to search out big bluestem—by late summer this grass will be waving its tiny flowers high above your head. Check out a tallgrass prairie in the fall, when the grasses turn shades of crimson and rust.

The mixed prairie looks much more layered and open. Forbs dot the landscape. You may see a dense stand of shrubs on a sheltered hillside. Look for little bluestem, one of the dominant grasses of this prairie. You will also see short grasses, such as buffalo grass, fescue, and grama grass. Don't miss the prairie dogs and bison herds!

In the spring and fall, the shortgrass prairie resembles a dense, gray-green turf. In the heat of the summer, the grasses dry up and the prairie turns tan. You'll see patches of bare soil between clumps of short grasses. After walking through this prairie, check your socks for the bristly seeds of buffalo grass and other plants. Spend some time at a prairie dog town or watching a herd of bison or pronghorns.

✔ Doing More

Take a step back in time. Read about the pioneers who crossed the prairie on the Oregon Trail or the Santa Fe Trail (see Appendix for suggested references). Visit areas where wagon ruts can still be seen or a sod house still stands. Some states such as Iowa and Nebraska have preserved such pioneer relics.

PROJECT **10**

Exploring Special Places II: Alpine Meadows

Picture yourself hiking a steep mountain trail. For hours you've been making your way through a dark, pungent forest of junipers and pines. Abruptly, you step out from under the forest canopy and into the sunlight. Brightly colored flowers set amidst a background of lush, green grass dazzle your eyes.

The meadow buzzes as bees busily visit flower after flower. With mountain peaks and a bright blue sky as background, the scene is stunning.

Although alpine meadows are but tiny parcels of grassland, they are well worth a visit. When exploring these special places, wear sturdy hiking boots. Carry a backpack with drinking water, snacks, and raingear for that likely afternoon thunderstorm. Include binoculars, a copy of the checklist shown below (Table 6), field guides to birds, wildflowers, and mammals, a camera and film, and your journal.

Alpine meadows can be found above timberline on any of the mountain ranges of the western and southwestern United States. Check out the Rocky Mountains, the Sierras, or the Cascades. Park rangers of the Forest Service or the National

---

Table 6   Checklist for Common Plants, Birds, and Mammals of Alpine Meadow

Plants
- ☐ Alpine fescue
- ☐ Alpine bluegrass
- ☐ Tufted hair grass
- ☐ Alpine timothy
- ☐ Spider woodrush
- ☐ Black sedge
- ☐ Ebony sedge
- ☐ Canada reedgrass
- ☐ Brewer's reedgrass
- ☐ Kentucky bluegrass
- ☐ Indian paintbrush
- ☐ Columbine
- ☐ Monkshood
- ☐ Monkey flower
- ☐ Elephant's head
- ☐ Glacier lily
- ☐ Shooting star
- ☐ Alpine aster
- ☐ Spreading phlox
- ☐ Alpine sunflower
- ☐ Jacob's ladder
- ☐ Alpine buttercup
- ☐ Snowball saxifrage
- ☐ Marsh marigold

Birds
- ☐ Rufous hummingbird
- ☐ Calliope hummingbird
- ☐ Lincoln's sparrow
- ☐ Golden eagle
- ☐ Red-tailed hawk
- ☐ White-tailed ptarmigan
- ☐ Willow ptarmigan
- ☐ Rock ptarmigan
- ☐ Northern harrier
- ☐ Peregrine falcon

Mammals
- ☐ Pocket gopher
- ☐ Mountain meadow mouse
- ☐ Belding's ground squirrel
- ☐ Mule deer
- ☐ Elk

Parks within these areas can direct you to specific hiking trails that afford the best views of mountain meadows.

Plan your visit around midsummer to view the peak of wildflower blooms. From April through October you will see wave after wave of different blossoms. In the spring, beware of soggy soils and melting snow banks. Mountain meadows are fragile ecosystems that are easily damaged by trampling. Keep on marked trails when exploring a meadow. Take only photographs of the plants or use a checklist to document your visit.

The species of plants and animals you'll find here differ greatly from those of the prairies. Expect to see more sedges and other grass-like plants. Look for mule deer or elk feeding in the meadow at dawn or dusk. Listen for the chirping of ground squirrels or chipmunks. Scan the sky for signs of a golden eagle or a red-tailed hawk.

✔ Doing More

In the eastern United States you can find other types of natural meadows. Conditions such as elevation, fire, temperature, and soil types create these grassy areas. Meadows known as balds are common in the higher elevations of the Appalachian Mountains. Several can be reached via trails in the Great Smoky Mountain National Park. In the northeast, check out the White Mountains of New Hampshire, the Green Mountains of Vermont, or the Adirondack Mountains of New York. What grasses and forbs are common to these eastern meadows?

PROJECT **11**
Exploring Special Places III: A Grassy Field

You don't have to scale a mountain or travel halfway across the country to find a grassland to explore. Step outside your front door or take a drive out of town. You'll see lawns and grassy fields aplenty. While these grasslands are mostly man-made habitats, they are easily accessible and offer good chances to study certain plants and animals up close.

To explore a field, you'll need garbage bags, a hand lens, binoculars, a long-shafted screwdriver, a shovel, a flashlight, red cellophane, a rubber band, field guides to grasses, wild-flowers, and weeds, a copy of the checklist below (Table 7), and your journal. You can find red cellophane at an arts and crafts supply shop. *Grassy fields can harbor chiggers and ticks! Wear long pants and thick socks to protect your legs.*

Once you've found a grassy field close to your home, ask the landowner's permission to study the field. Be sure to mention if you are interested in collecting plant or animal specimens. Once you have approval, gather your equipment. Spend some time at the field getting to know the plants that grow

---

Table 7   Checklist for Common Plants, Birds, and Mammals of Eastern Grassy Fields

Plants
- ☐ Timothy
- ☐ Kentucky bluegrass
- ☐ Tall fescu
- ☐ Orchard grass
- ☐ Smooth brome
- ☐ Red top
- ☐ Broomsedge
- ☐ Johnson grass
- ☐ Common milkweed
- ☐ Queen Anne's lace
- ☐ Oxeye daisy
- ☐ Shasta daisy
- ☐ White sweet clover
- ☐ Yellow sweet clover
- ☐ Red clover
- ☐ White clover
- ☐ Yarrow
- ☐ Common sunflower
- ☐ Thistle
- ☐ Black-eyed Susan

Birds
- ☐ Killdeer
- ☐ Barn swallow
- ☐ Eastern meadowlark
- ☐ Grasshopper sparrow
- ☐ Field sparrow
- ☐ Savannah sparrow
- ☐ American goldfinch

Mammals
- ☐ Meadow vole
- ☐ Field mouse
- ☐ Raccoon
- ☐ Skunk
- ☐ Opossum
- ☐ Fox
- ☐ White-tailed deer
- ☐ Cotton-tailed rabbit

there. Use the checklist on the previous page to guide you as well as to document your discoveries.

To view the wildlife, plan a trip to the field just before dawn or at dusk. Bring along a flashlight. Wrap a piece of red cellophane around the head of the flashlight, using a rubber band to keep the cellophane in place. The red beam will allow you to see the animals without frightening them. Enter the field quietly and find a place to sit. What animals visit the field? What do they do while in the field?

✔ Doing More

Don't overlook the grassland just outside your front door. Get down on your hands and knees and check out a lawn. Can you find the stems, nodes, blades, and flowers of a grass plant (see Project 3)? Look for runners or **stolons**. These are especially easy to see along a driveway's edge. Dig into the soil to look for rhizomes. Use a guidebook on lawns to help you identify the grasses. Common lawn grasses include zoysia, Bermuda, St. Augustine, fescue, Kentucky bluegrass, and ryegrass. What other plants grow in or near the lawn?

As you examine the plants, look for signs of animals. You may see ants, jumping spiders, crickets, small burrows, mole crickets, half-eaten acorns, or rabbit pellets. Look for earthworms or their burrows. Use a shovel to cut into the turf. Pull the blade back to view a section of earth. Do you see tunnels or small holes beneath the surface?

CHAPTER 3

Creatures of The Prairie

EARLY PRAIRIE EXPLORERS OFTEN COM-pared the prairie to the ocean. Pioneers crossing the prairie called their wagons prairie schooners, after the sailing boats of the 18th century. Picture yourself traveling on a 21st century prairie schooner that could float just above the tops of the grasses. Clinging to the side of the vessel as it gently rides the swells and dips of the grassland, what animals would you see?

Adorning the top of the grassy sea, showy prairie flowers attract humming-birds, butterflies, moths, beetles, wasps, bees, and even flies. A crab spider may be camouflaged among the petals, intently studying the activity. Don't overlook the tops of the grassy stalks. Here you may see a praying mantis waiting to make a kill or a male songbird looking for a mate.

Other songsters can be heard from the depths of the grasses. Listen for the buz-zing and rasping of grasshoppers, crick-ets, locusts, and katydids. If you wade through the grasses, you're sure to scare up a few of these creatures. Look for smaller, quieter insects like caterpillars, ants, aphids, and leafhoppers. You'll often find them crawling up and down stems or over leaves in search of something to eat.

Deep down in the grasses, on the floor of the sea of grass, live many small mammals and ground-nesting birds. Mice, rats, voles, and shrews make this place their home. The feet of these tiny rodents beat pathways into the ground, while their sharp teeth clip tunnels through the grass. In the spring, birds, such as the meadowlark, bobolink, or grasshopper sparrow, build their nests on the ground. Look for small, scooped-out depressions hidden in the grasses.

By far the most populated habitat of the prairie ocean is the underworld—a dark, dense world of soil and tangled roots. Small organisms like bacteria, **protozoans**, fungi, **nematodes**, earthworms, and ants, as well as larger animals such as prairie dogs, pocket gophers, moles, badgers, and ground squirrels inhabit this realm. Dig into the soil to find earthworms and nematodes. Search for mounds of excavated earth, holes in the ground, or a line of pushed-up soil—all signs of the activities of some underworld prairie creature.

Some prairie animals are easy to spot. It's hard to miss a bison that weighs almost a ton! Another large animal of the plains is the pronghorn, an animal related to the antelope. The pronghorn, North America's swiftest mammal, can dance across the prairie at speeds up to 112 kilometers per hour (70 mph).

Circling high above you may see birds of prey like the golden eagle, Swainson's hawk, American kestrel, prairie falcon, Northern harrier, or ferruginous hawk. Just one of these predators may consume hundreds of rodents in a spring and summer.

If you search in all these places, you're sure to discover prairie creatures you haven't seen before. Use the activities that follow to learn more about grassland animals. Visit a prairie preserve to observe the bigger animals like

*The pronghorn ante-
lope lives in the
prairies. Running at
speeds up to 112
kilometers per hour
(70 mph), it is North
America's swiftest
mammal.*

prairie dogs, bison, and pronghorns. Keep a list to record the animals you encounter on your prairie voyages.

Butterflies Revisited:
What You Didn't Learn in Kindergarten

Can you remember how you felt when you first saw a caterpillar turn into a butterfly? If your memory is a little dim, here's your chance to take a second look at the wondrous life cycle of these beautiful creatures. Butterflies love sunny, open fields with lots of wildflowers, so you're sure to run across them in your prairie explorations.

Gather a hand lens, scissors, field guides to butterflies, wildflowers, and trees (see Appendix for suggested references), and your journal. Make an insect rearing cage using the materials and instructions given in the Appendix.

Are you ready to hunt eggs? Brace yourself. This won't be as easy as hunting Easter eggs. Most butterfly eggs are about the size of the head of a straight pin. But they're really not that hard to find, if you look in the right places. Female butterflies are very picky about where they lay their eggs. Most lay their eggs on only a few kinds of plants. The plants that support the egg and developing caterpillar are called larval host plants. Check Table 8 on page 55 for a list of common butterflies and their host plants.

Look for a few of these host plants in your yard, garden, neighborhood, or nearby park. When you find one, search the top and bottom surfaces of young leaves for a tiny egg. Most butterfly eggs are white, yellow, or even pale green. Study the egg with your hand lens. Sketch the egg in your journal.

If you come up empty-handed, try enticing the butterflies to lay their eggs in your own backyard. Buy some larval host plants from a nursery. Be sure to purchase several of the same kind. A cluster of parsley plants is more likely than a single plant to attract an egg-laying swallowtail. Place the plants in a sunny spot in your yard. Water them frequently. From

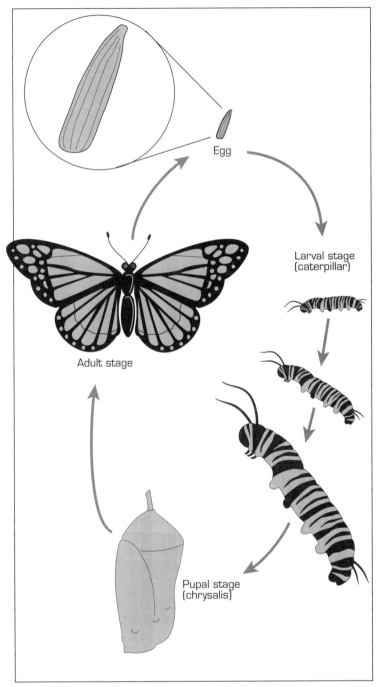

Figure 11 Butterfly Life Cycle

Table 8   Where to Find Butterfly Eggs

If you Locate This Plant:	Look for the Eggs or Caterpillars of This Butterfly:
Trees	
Aspen	Viceroy, Mourning cloak, Admirals
Birch	Mourning cloak, White Admiral
Cherry	Tiger swallowtail, Spring azure
Citrus	Anise swallowtail, Giant swallowtail
Cottonwood	Viceroy, Mourning cloak, Admirals
Dogwood	Spring azure
Elm	Comma, Mourning cloak
Hackberry	Question mark, Tawny Emperor
Locust	Silver-spotted skipper
Oak	Sister, Banded hairstreak
Pawpaw	Zebra swallowtail
Sassafras	Tiger or Spicebush swallowtail
Tulip popular	Tiger swallowtail
Willow	Western admiral, Viceroy
Wild forbs	
Aster	Pearl crescent
Clover	Clouded sulphur, Eastern tailed blue
Everlasting	American painted lady
False indigo	Silver-spotted skipper, Dog face
False nettle	Red admiral, Comma, Question mark
Lupine	Silvery blue
Mallow	West Coast lady, Gray hairstreak
Milk vetch	Western tailed blue
Milkweed	Monarch, Queen
Nettle	Red admiral, Question mark, Comma
Queen Anne's lace	Black or Anise swallowtail
Vetch	Alfalfa sulphur, Eastern tailed blue
Garden plants	
Alfalfa	Clouded sulphur, Eastern tailed blue
Bean	Long-tailed skipper
Broccoli	Cabbage white, Checkered white
Cabbage	Cabbage white, Checkered white
Marigold	Dainty sulphur
Parsley	Black or Anise swallowtail
Sweet fennel	Anise or Black swallowtail
Winter cress	Sara orange tip, Cabbage white

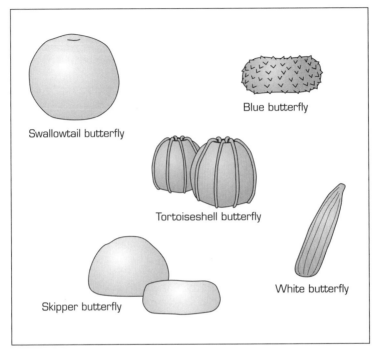

Blue butterfly

Swallowtail butterfly

Tortoiseshell butterfly

White butterfly

Skipper butterfly

Figure 12 Butterfly Eggs

spring through fall, butterflies will be laying eggs. Watch for adults flittering around the plants. If you are lucky, you might even see a female laying an egg!

When you finally find an egg, collect it along with a short section of stem. Wrap the cut end of the plant in a wet paper towel and bring it inside. Place the plant cutting in the insect rearing cage as described in the Appendix. Replace the lid of the cage. Set the cage in a sunny room but away from direct sunlight.

Check the egg daily. Most species hatch within 4 to 7 days. The first meal that the caterpillar eats is often the egg case itself!

After that first meal, the caterpillar will want fresh, young leaves every day. Use only leaves of the same plant species on which you found the egg. To be certain that your tiny captive is eating, look for half-eaten leaves and droppings or frass. Replace soiled paper towels daily.

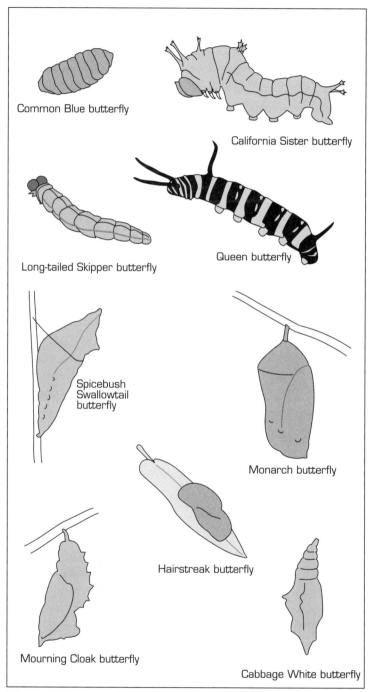

Common Blue butterfly

California Sister butterfly

Long-tailed Skipper butterfly

Queen butterfly

Spicebush
Swallowtail
butterfly

Monarch butterfly

Hairstreak butterfly

Mourning Cloak butterfly

Cabbage White butterfly

Figure 13 Butterfly Caterpillars and Chrysalids

Sometime during the second week, the caterpillar will stop eating. It will begin crawling around, looking for a place to **pupate**. Put a few woody sticks in the cage. Soon your caterpillar will stop moving, find a place to attach, and spin a silken covering around its body. If one day you suddenly can't find it, check up under the lid.

Observe the pupa often. Within two weeks, you'll see the butterfly crawl out of its casing. Notice how small the newly emerged butterfly first appears. Keep watching, for soon it will pump its wings and expand to full size. Ask a young child to help you release it. He or she will love watching the butterfly on its maiden voyage.

✔ Doing More

Plant a butterfly garden (see Appendix for references). Learn the names of the butterflies that live in your area. Use a butterfly net to observe them up close, but treat them gently and release them when you're through. Would you like to help scientists study monarch migration? Contact Monarch Watch for information on the project. Their address is listed in the Appendix.

INVESTIGATION **1**

Hordes of Hungry, Hopping Herbivores

From tender, green leaves to seeds, fruits, and even roots, a grassland presents quite a smorgasbord to hungry herbivores. Bison, elk, pronghorns, rodents, ground squirrels, rabbits, hares, birds, insects, and nematodes all dine on the grasses and forbs. Few of these animals are more voracious consumers than the grasshoppers. While a single grasshopper might not seem to eat much, hordes of them can mow the grasses to the ground.

How many grasshoppers inhabit the grassland you've been exploring? To find out, collect red nail polish, a sweep net, toothpicks, several stakes, surveyor's flagging or strips of bright fabric, several friends, and your journal. ***Bring plenty of water, wear a hat, and wear long pants and thick socks to protect against ticks and chiggers.*** Be sure to ask permission from the landowner if you will be working on private property. Buy a sweep net from a biological supply house or make your own using the directions given in the Appendix.

By capturing a small sample of the grasshopper population, marking the captives with a dot of nail polish, releasing them, then re-sampling the population a few days later, you can estimate the size of the population. The number of re-captured, marked individuals is mathematically related to the size of the total population, as shown in the following equation.

$$\text{Population Size} = \frac{(\text{total no. hoppers captured in 2nd sweep}) (\text{no. hoppers marked in 1st sweep})}{(\text{no. recaptured, marked hoppers in 2nd sweep})}$$

Collect grasshoppers in late summer through early fall. By then, the insects will have reached their adult size and will be easier to catch. Can you tell the difference between a grasshopper, a cricket, or other hopping insects? If you can't, study a field guide first.

Start your survey at one corner of a prairie or field. Mark the site with a stake and flagging. Assign everyone a job—one person to work the sweep net, one person to hold the grasshopper, one person to mark it, and someone to keep track of the number of marked grasshoppers.

Swing the sweep net back and forth, beating the grasses as you walk. After several strokes of the net, check the bag for captives, then close off the opening by grabbing the net below the hoop. Make a small opening through which you can quickly snatch an insect out of the net. Keep the net closed to retain the other captives. Hold the insect by firmly pressing its thighs (femurs) up against its body. Mark the back (thorax) of the grasshopper with a dab of nail polish on the end of a toothpick. Allow the polish to dry, record using a tally mark in your chart, and release the insect. Mark the remaining grasshoppers in your net using the same method.

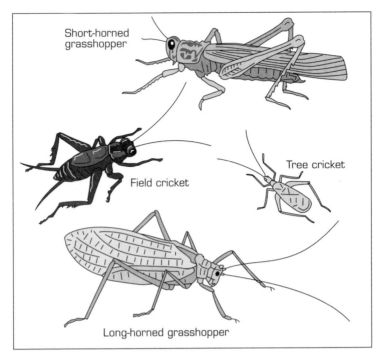

Figure 14 Grasshoppers and Crickets

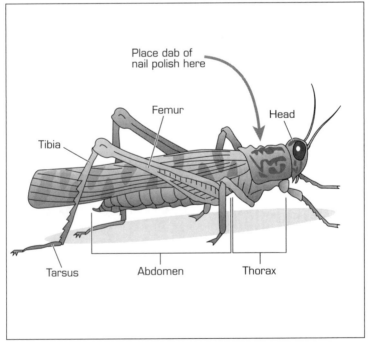

Figure 15 Parts of a Grasshopper

Work your way across and down the field, until at least 50 grasshoppers have been marked and released. Do not mark any grasshopper twice.

Return within the week to resweep the field with the net. Record the number of marked and unmarked grasshoppers that you catch. Continue until you have captured at least 50 grasshoppers. Estimate the total grasshopper population using the equation on the previous page. You may see about 30 grasshoppers per square meter (or 3 per square ft.), but grasshopper populations increase dramatically during a prolonged drought.

PROJECT **13**

Discovering Eight-Legged Hunters

Not all hunters rely on piercing fangs, razor-sharp claws, powerful muscles, or great speed to capture their prey. Spiders may have piercing fangs, but it is their ability to make silk and weave it into unusual snares and traps that sets them apart from other hunting animals. Many of these small hunters live in prairies, fields, and meadows.

While you may have to search hard to find spiders, you can more easily locate their webs. For this project, you'll need a spray bottle or mister, a flashlight, a pencil, your journal, and a field guide to spiders. ***Although most spiders aren't harmful, play it safe. Make sure you can identify any poisonous spiders, such as the black widow spider and the brown recluse, that live in the area you'll be exploring***.

Find a prairie or grassy field to explore. Because most spiders die before winter, plan your trip in summer or fall. Pick a dry day several days after a rain. While you can see spiders almost any time of the day, try to be in the field very early in the morning, even before dawn. Plan on visiting again at night, using a bright flashlight. You may be lucky enough to watch a spider repairing its web!

The silken threads of a web are only a few micrometers

This black and white argiope, commonly found in meadows, is repairing its web.

($\frac{1}{100}$ in.) in diameter and are almost transparent. Still, they're not invisible. As you walk through a field, move toward the light to get your best views of any webs. Crouch down to scan the tops of the grasses at a different angle. If the silken threads catch the light, you'll see them glint and sparkle.

In tall grasses, look for large, circular webs hanging vertically between the stalks. These webs are called orb webs. Study the intricate pattern of one for a minute. To make each tiny thread stand out, mist the web gently with water. Do you see a spider on the web or hiding nearby? Touch the web lightly with the tip of your pencil. How does the spider react?

In short grasses, look for smaller, sheet-like webs carpeting the ground. Some will have a funnel-shaped opening in the center that leads down into the grass or between some rocks. If you peer closely into the funnel, you may catch a glimpse of its owner. If you can, squeeze the funnel's lower end to scare the spider out of seclusion.

A third type of web, the sheet web, can be found laid out across the grass or tucked between the branches and leaves of a shrub or tree. A sheet web consists of a densely woven platform about 15 centimeters (6 in.) wide, held in place by several thin, guy lines. The spider waits beneath for an unwary insect to be tripped up by the almost invisible support threads. Try dropping a live beetle onto the web. How does the spider respond?

✔ Doing More
Not all spiders spin webs to snare their prey. The crab spider ambushes its prey. Perched on a flower, this spider sits well in sight of any of its prey. Because the spider changes its color to match its surroundings, it is seldom noticed until too late. Look for this spider on white or yellow flowers of the daisy family. Watch what happens when a bee or fly visits the flower.

PROJECT 14

Bird Watching in a Sea of Grass

In the spring, a grassland bursts into flower and into song. As migrating birds return, set up territories, court, and mate, cheery whistles, trills, and bubbling melodies can be heard issuing from fence posts and grassy stalks.

Who are these feathered musicians? To find out, grab a pair of binoculars, a field guide to birds, and your journal. With just these and a few tips on observing grassland birds, you'll be well on your way to an exciting, birding adventure.

If you've never used binoculars to spot wildlife, practice before you visit a grassland. An experienced birdwatcher first watches a bird with just her eyes. Keeping her eyes on the bird, she lifts the binoculars to her face to get a better view. Try this procedure to view birds in your backyard or at a nearby park.

To see the greatest variety of birds, plan your birding trip during or after the spring migrations and before or during fall migration—by late May and then again in late August or September. Find a prairie or a large, grassy field. Seek the landowner's permission if the land is privately owned. ***Wear long***

pants to protect against ticks and chiggers! Plan your birding trip for dawn or late afternoon. The birds will be more active during these times and you will have an easier time
spotting them.

Because loud noises cause most birds to seek cover, walk
as quietly as you can. Stop often. Keep talk to a minimum. Listen instead. If you hear a call, can you locate the singer?

Keep an eye out for the darting movement of a bird as it
flies from one perch to another. Good perches include fence
posts, telephone poles, living trees, large dead trees, shrubs,
grass stalks, and wildflower stems. Many grassland birds prefer to remain hidden among the grasses. You're sure to flush
out a few as you stroll along. As a bird drops to a new ground
site, observe its general size, color, the shape and size of its
bill, as well as any special markings. These features will help
you identify the bird using a field guide.

Do you see any birds of prey circling in the sky or perched
on telephone poles or fence poles? Notice the shape of the
wings as they fly. If you wait long enough, you may catch one
of these predators in action, swooping down on an unsus-
pecting prairie vole or other small animal.

Keep a list of the birds that you spot. Record the date of
the sighting and the location, including town and state, in your
journal. If you are visiting a prairie preserve, you may be able
to pick up a checklist of birds from a ranger or the park office. Look over the checklists provided in Projects 9 and 11
for lists of common birds of prairies and grassy fields.

✔ Doing More

Learn to identify grassland birds by their calls even while they
remain hidden in the grasses. Check out a library or book-
store for audiotapes or compact discs with birdsongs
recorded on them to help you.

Holes in the Ground:
Investigating Small Mammal Hideouts

The floor of a grassland is riddled with holes, cavities, and tunnels. Some holes are yawning cavities marked by huge mounds of earth, while others are tiny, finger-sized openings hidden among grassy stalks. Large or small, all lead to the homes and byways of small, grassland animals.

Finding the entrance to a burrow is just the beginning of the mystery. Next you need to figure out who lives down that hole. Try your hand at a little detective work. With a little luck and lots of patience, you might even meet the creature face to face.

For this activity, you'll need a pole or walking stick to push aside tall grasses and shrubs, surveyor's flagging or strips of fabric, a broom, a flashlight, a tape measure, binoculars, a field guide to mammals, a field guide to animal signs and tracks, and your journal. *A grassland can get quite hot and abound with ticks and chiggers. Be safe! Take plenty of water, wear a hat and sunscreen, and protect your legs with socks and long pants.*

Grassland mammals are most active around dawn and dusk, from spring through fall. Because visibility is limited at dusk and dense plant cover later in the growing season will obscure many burrows, plan to do your burrow sleuthing at dawn on a spring or early summer day.

Choose a prairie or grassy field for your search. Sketch a rough map in your journal. Systematically walk the area, keeping your eyes on the ground. Use your pole or walking stick to bend stems and branches aside. Search for holes (some may be plugged during the day), mounds, and other signs of freshly dug soil. Some burrows may lie along prominent trails or runways. Double-check areas within dense clumps of grasses, underneath the hanging limbs of shrubs, or on small mounds or rises. Large mammals often place their burrows on slopes or in breaks along hillsides.

When you find a burrow opening, tie a piece of flagging

to a plant near by and mark the spot on your map. Measure the size of the hole and note the shape of the opening. ***Never put your hand or your head inside a burrow! Wasps, bees, venomous spiders, and venomous snakes sometimes inhabit burrows.*** Carefully examine the ground around the burrow for clues to the burrow's inhabitants. Look for tracks, droppings, small bones, and signs of freshly dug dirt. ***Do not handle the droppings because they may contain parasites.*** Record your observations in your journal.

Continue your walk. As you stroll, listen for the squeaks, trills, or whistles of small mammals. Examine every burrow you come across, noting the location in your journal.

When you've found several burrows, it's time to stop and think. Who lives in each of these underground burrows or dens? To answer this question, first look over Table 9 on the next page. Next, consult a field guide to mammals to check range maps, burrow sizes and shapes, and other signs. Keep in mind that the size of the burrow opening is usually proportional to the size of the animal. For example, mice burrows may be only 3 centimeters (1 in.) in diameter, ground squirrel burrows about 7 centimeters (3 in.), and prairie dog and badger homes up to 30 centimeters (12 in.).

Follow up your reading with a burrow stakeout at dawn. Bring along binoculars and plenty of patience. Find a spot downwind, behind the burrow opening and out of view, but close enough to observe any creatures that might emerge. A clump of tall grass or nearby shrub makes a good blind. Get into a comfortable position that you can maintain for 30 minutes or longer without moving. Keep your eyes focused on the burrow opening. When an animal appears, notice its size, color, and any facial or body markings. Keep a record of the animal's behavior. These notes will help you identify it later using a field guide.

If you aren't lucky enough to spot a burrower, perhaps you are staking out an abandoned burrow. Do you see spider webs, leaves, or other debris around the opening? If not, before you leave for the night, sweep the area around the burrow. Return the next day to look for fresh tracks. If no tracks are visible, assume the burrow is abandoned. Select another

---

Table 9   Burrowing Mammals of Prairies and Eastern Grasslands (Fields, Pastures, Hay Meadows)

Badger
Woodchuck
Eastern mole
Striped skunk
Coyote (den use in spring to raise pups)
Red fox (den use in spring to raise pups)
Swift fox (year-round den use)
White-tailed prairie dog
Black-tailed prairie dog
Thirteen-lined ground squirrel
Richardson's ground squirrel
Franklin's ground squirrel
Spotted ground squirrel
Plains pocket gopher
Ord's kangaroo rat
Oldfield mouse
Deer mouse
Fulvous harvest mouse
Northern grasshopper mouse
Southern grasshopper mouse
Plains pocket mouse
Olive-backed pocket mouse
Prairie vole

---

one to stake out. Remember, the key to burrow watching is patience. Sooner or later you'll be rewarded!

PROJECT **16**

Using a Baermann Funnel to Extract Soil Animals

Plant-eaters love the succulent shoots, tender leaves, and crunchy, juicy stems that a grassland provides. But some of the most abundant herbivores live, not above ground, but below ground, feeding on the miles of roots that prairie grasses and forbs send into the soil. Up to a half million of these animals may live in $\frac{1}{10}$ of a square meter (1 square ft.) of prairie earth.

What kind of animals are these? Worms! Not earthworms, but roundworms or nematodes. To view these tiny creatures, you'll need the following: a funnel; rubber tubing; a pinch clamp or clothespin; a support stand; ring and clamps; facial tissues; string; an aluminum screening or hardware cloth; tin snips; a watch glass or custard cup; a shovel; a resealable plastic sandwich bag; a permanent marker; a dissecting microscope or hand lens; water; and your journal.

Scientists pull nematodes out of the soil using a special device called a Baermann funnel. From some simple supplies, you can make one yourself. First attach a 15-centimeter (6-in.) piece of tubing to the spout end of a funnel. Close the free end of tubing with a clothespin or pinch clamp. Using tin snips, cut a small circle of metal screening just large enough to set inside the funnel opening above the spout. Place the screening in the funnel. Now support the funnel with a ring clamped to a ring stand.

In a prairie or grassy field, dig to a depth of 8 to 13 centimeters (3 to 5 in.) to collect a soil sample. Store the sample in a resealable plastic bag. When you get home, refrigerate the sample until you're ready to extract the nematodes.

Begin the extraction by placing a handful of the soil sample in the center of a double layer of facial tissues. Lift the corners of the square and bring them together. Tie the corners with string to form a make-shift bag.

Fill the Baermann funnel half-full of water. Place the wrapped soil in the water. The soil bundle should be partially submerged. The soil nematodes will slowly wriggle their way out of the soil and drop to the bottom of the funnel. They will accumulate just above the clamp on the rubber tubing. After 24 to 48 hours, open the pinch clamp. Collect 10 drops of water in a watch glass or custard cup. Set the container on a dark surface and look for transparent, slender, round worms with a hand lens or dissecting microscope. Scan the

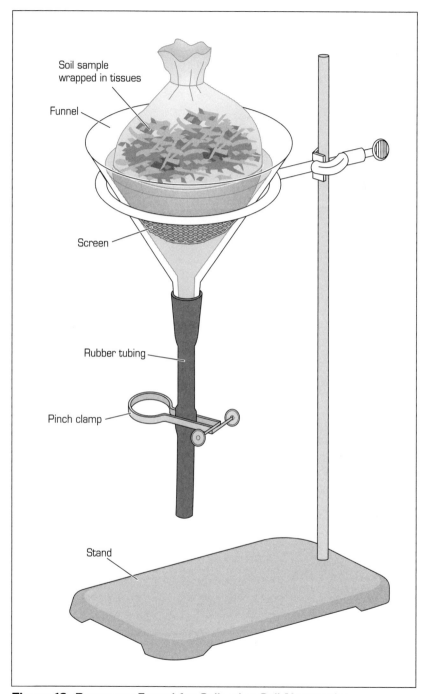

Figure 16 Baermann Funnel for Collecting Soil Nematodes

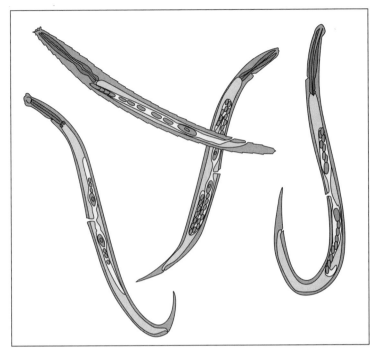

Figure 17 Soil Nematodes

collection jar carefully. Most soil nematodes are between 0.1 and 100 millimeters (0.004 and 4.0 in.) in length. Unlike earthworms, nematode bodies are not segmented. They move by bending or flipping their bodies. How many kinds of nematodes do you see?

CHAPTER 4

Living in The Land of Extremes

IF THE WEATHER GIVES YOU FITS IN your neck of the woods, just imagine if you were a mouse living on the prairie. Here summer temperatures can soar to a sweltering 48°C (118°F). Winters hit with bone-chilling numbness as temperatures plummet to –51°C (–60°F). Sometimes temperatures drop 11° to 22°C (20° to 40°F) in a single day!

That's not the worst of it. High above the prairie, westerly winds collide with artic air masses and tropical airstreams, creating violent storms. Late afternoon summer thunderstorms bring torrential rains, lightning, thunder, and gusts of wind up to 160 kilometers per hour (100 miles per hour). Tornadoes blow through with wild, cyclonic winds of up to 480 kilo-meters per hour (300 miles per hour). Blizzards combine fierce winds with blinding snow and frigid cold.

These won't be your only worries. The

unpredictable nature of rainfall could leave your food source wilting or dying. Total rainfall on the prairie can fluctuate as much as two- to three-fold from year to year. Extended dry periods often occur during the growing season. A drought can last 6 or 7 weeks, or longer! But in some years, floods wash over the prairie.

During dry periods, summer thunderstorms crackle and boom, sending fire strikes into tinder-dry grasses. Scientists believe that, before European settlers arrived, fire scorched any part of the prairie at least once every 3 to 5 years.

What a challenging place to live! How do prairie creatures survive? How do prairie plants, rooted to the earth, manage to live in such a place? Both prairie plants and animals show many adaptations to their environment—in their structures, in the way their bodies function, and in their behaviors.

Many prairie creatures tunnel into the soil to escape the harshness of the weather. In the heat of the summer, a burrow offers cooler temperatures, while a nest lined with fur, leaves, or fluffy seeds can be quite toasty in the cold, winter months. These underground homes also provide respite from wind, rain, hail, or a racing fire line.

Not all animals, though, can dig a burrow. Some borrow abandoned burrows. Others clip grass stems to make small, dome-shaped nests. Many insects and spiders climb up and down stems and leaves to stay cool or warm up.

While plants aren't capable of much movement, they do have ways of beating the prairie weather. In the winter, most prairie plant life goes underground. Only the roots and underground stems live through these hard times. In the summer, a prairie plant's biggest problem is water loss. Although some animals can survive without taking in water, plants cannot. They wilt and die when too much water is lost from their tissues. Most of this water loss occurs through tiny openings in leaves and stems called **stomata**. In some forbs, tiny hairs surround the stomata. These hairs, called **trichomes**, reflect light and keep water from escaping. Grasses use another method to reduce water loss or transpiration. A grass leaf often has a center fold along the blade. Special cells fold the leaf during high heat or drought, thus covering the stomata and slowing water loss.

Life on the prairie can be pretty hard. Use the activities in this chapter to see just how tough prairie weather really is. Explore a few of the ways prairie animals and plants have adapted to life in the land of extremes.

INVESTIGATION **2**

Nature's Ups and Downs: Changing Temperatures and Insect Positioning in the Grasses

Insects don't sweat and they can't shiver. When it gets very hot or too cool, the best these cold-blooded animals can do is move. They shift to a sunny or shaded spot, crouch down on the ground, crawl up or down a grassy stalk, or even burrow into the soil.

In an open landscape like a field or prairie, air temperatures change dramatically over the course of a day. Find out firsthand how much temperatures change and watch how grasshoppers respond to such temperature shifts. You'll need a three-tiered vertical holder (see Appendix for directions to make your own), several thermometers, binoculars, copies of the data sheets provided here (Table 10 and Table 11), and your journal.

First construct the vertical holder using the directions given in the Appendix. Don't forget to perform the thermometer checks described there.

Next scout around for a nearby grassy field or prairie. Once you've selected a good site, obtain landowner permission to do your studies. Plan your outing for a sunny, summer day.

Gather your equipment and gear. ***Wear long pants to protect your legs against chiggers and ticks***. ***Pack plenty***

Table 10 Temperature Data Sheet

Note: Hr = hour; Temp A = temperature at ground level; Temp B = temperature at 1/2 meter; Temp C = temperature at tops of the grasses. Record temperatures on the hour throughout the day.

Name of Observer: _____

Date: _____

Weather Conditions (circle those that apply):

Sunny   Partly cloudy   Overcast   Windy   Breezy   Calm   Mist   Light rain   Heavy rain

Hr	Temp A	Temp B	Temp C

Table 11 Grasshopper Observation Data Sheet

Note: GH = grasshopper; Gr = ground; Bl = blade; Cu = culm or stem; Cr = crouching; Fl = flanking; Sh = shading; Su = sunning; St = stilting. At the half hour, record the location and posture of each grasshopper in your vicinity. View the insects with binoculars, if necessary. Use abbreviations given above to record your observations. Separate data for each grasshopper using a double slashed line.

Name of Observer: _____

Date: _____

Hour	Time	Observations

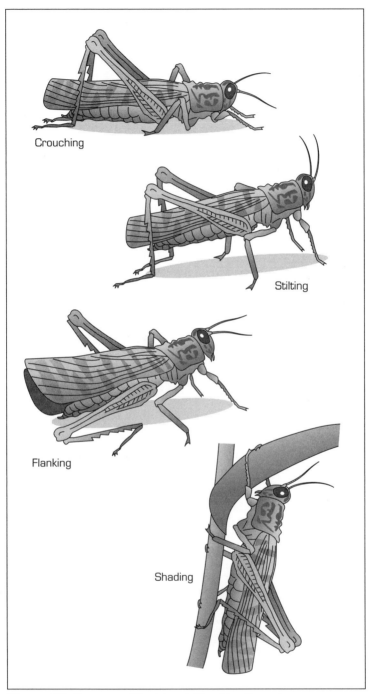

Crouching

Stilting

Flanking

Shading

Figure 18 Postures (Positions) Used by Grasshoppers to Regulate Their Body Temperatures

of water and food. Don't forget to bring sunscreen and wear a hat! Head to the site early in the morning. Set the vertical holder upright in the ground and place a thermometer in each holder. Position one holder at ground level, a second at 50 centimeters (20 in.), and the third at the tops of the grasses. Record the height of this last holder in your journal. Find a comfortable place close by from which you can observe grasshoppers. When alarmed, the grasshoppers will take flight, so settle in quickly. They should resume their normal activities within 30 minutes.

Take temperature readings on the hour, through the afternoon or evening. Between temperature readings, observe grasshopper behavior, recording observations at the half hour. Note such information as location of grasshoppers (ground versus plant stem or blade), and body postures (crouching, stilting, flanking, and shading). Study the figures on the previous page to familiarize yourself with these different postures.

What does your data tell you about daily temperature cycles in an open landscape? At what height above the ground did the air temperature fluctuate the most? How do grasshoppers adapt to these changing temperatures?

✔ Doing More

If you live outside the prairie states and are curious about daily temperature cycles on the prairie, log onto the National Climate Data Center's Web site at http://www.ncdc.noaa .gov/. From their home page, click on *Climate Resources*, then go to *Get/View Climate Data*. Scan down to *Surface Data Hourly*, then *U.S. Select by Station*. Choose *Unedited Local Climate Data* for a summer month.

Rain, Rain, Come Again: Retrieving Rainfall Data of the Prairie Using the Internet

The poet Emily Dickinson once wrote that, to make a prairie, it takes one clover and a bee. A scientist might say that climate makes a prairie—a little rain, lots of sun, and plenty of drought. It may not sound as poetic, but it's a little nearer to the truth!

You can investigate this idea without ever leaving your chair. Forget about setting up rain gauges or a simple weather station. Let the National Weather Service do the work. All you need to do is go online to retrieve the data. You'll also need a map of the United States and your journal.

Visit the National Climate Data Center's (NCDC) Web site. Type in the address *www.ncdc.noaa.gov*. From their home page, click on *Climate Resources*. On that page, you will be offered a number of options. Select *Get/View Online Climate Data*. Now scroll down the page to find the heading *Surface Data: Graphs and Maps*. Click on *Climate Visualization or CLIMVIS*. Once you're at the CLIMVIS page, choose the option to view the *Time Series for Climate Division Drought Data*. At this point you should have reached the *Graphing Options* page. Where you go from here depends on the questions you are asking.

If you want to compare rainfall data for a forest, desert, and prairie, click on *Display the Period of Record for a Parameter*. This will allow you to select an area of a state and the type of data that you wish to view. The period of record represents the years for which the Climate Data Center has data.

Confused about which areas of the country to select? Forests cover much of the eastern United States. Try looking at Massachusetts, for example. The Center puts each state into two or more divisions. You can view and even print out their maps showing the divisions by number. To locate a prairie state, check the map in the Introduction of this book. To view data for a desert, select a division in the lower third of Arizona.

Once you've selected the state division, choose the parameter to view (precipitation), then click on *Generate the*

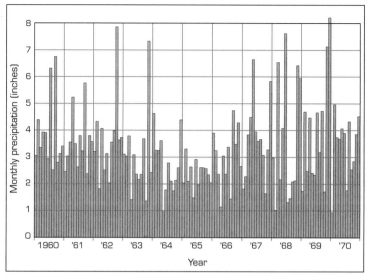

Figure 19 **Massachusetts Forest Rainfall**

Graph. Print out each set of data and label the graphs as forest, desert, or prairie. Be sure to label all graph axes.

Now return to *Graphing Options.* By choosing *Display All Divisions for a State, Year, and Parameter*, you can look at monthly rainfall data for a given year for any part of a state. Take a careful look at the first graph that you generated for the prairie. Do you see any years that seem particularly dry or wet? Select one of those years. Generate the graph using *Display All Divisions for a State, Year and Parameter* and print it. Do the same for forest data and desert data.

Take a minute to study the graphs you just printed. How different are the patterns and total amount of precipitation that fall on a prairie, forest, or desert? For each ecosystem, is the precipitation evenly distributed throughout a year or confined to just a few months? Within a prairie region, how variable is the pattern of precipitation from year to year?

✔ **Doing More**

A great drought hit southwestern Kansas and the surrounding states in the 1930's. High winds created terrible dust storms that lasted for days, earning that part of the country

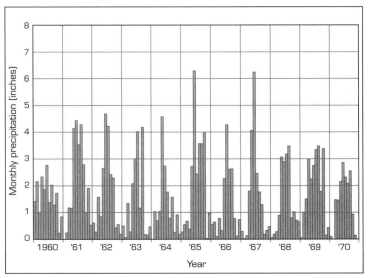

Figure 20 Kansas Prairie Rainfall

the nickname of the Dust Bowl. Use the World Wide Web to investigate the weather conditions during those years. Read pioneer accounts of drought and dust storms (see Appendix).

Observing Plant Hairs with a Hand Lens

The heat from a blistering prairie summer day sends most animals scurrying into a burrow or seeking the coolness of a den. Prairie plants have evolved other ways of dealing with the heat. Some prairie plants cover their leaves and stems with hairs. Plant hairs or trichomes can be found on leaves, stems, flowers, and seed coats. They range from hundredths of a millimeter to several millimeters (thousandths of an inch to tenths of an inch) in length and take on many different shapes and forms. Some are short and tapered while others exhibit complex branching patterns. Trichomes reflect solar radiation, lower leaf temperature, and lower rates of water loss.

To view these unusual structures, you'll need a hand lens, a piece of brightly colored ribbon, your journal, and a field guide to wildflowers and grasses. Tie a piece of ribbon to the hand lens. This will help you spot it if you drop it in the grasses.

Grab your lens, journal, and field guides. Find a nearby grassy field or prairie to visit. Search out black-eyed Susan, bush clover, common mullein or other plants whose leaves appear fuzzy, woolly, or silver-gray. ***Watch out for stinging nettle! This plant is covered with tiny hairs, each of which is filled with formic acid and can deliver a sharp pain when touched.*** Leaves without trichomes appear dark, shiny, and smooth. Examine all surfaces of the leaves, stems, and flowers. Note the thickness and denseness of the hairs. Which leaves appear to be better adapted to the prairie climate?

✔ Doing More

Water loss is a major problem for plants that live in hot, dry climates. Much of the water is lost through tiny openings called stomata in leaves and stems. With a hand lens or dissecting microscope, tweezers, and clear nail polish, you can actually see these openings. Paint the undersurface of a leaf with nail polish. For the best effect, select leaves with few or no hairs. Let the polish dry. Carefully peel off the polish and view it using a microscope. Look for tiny holes—these are the stomata.

Wildfire: Prairie Style

The Native Americans called it red buffalo. It raced over the plains, sometimes covering 200 kilometers (120 mi.) in a day's time, pushed on by the constant winds. The sound carried great distances as the fire roared and thundered across

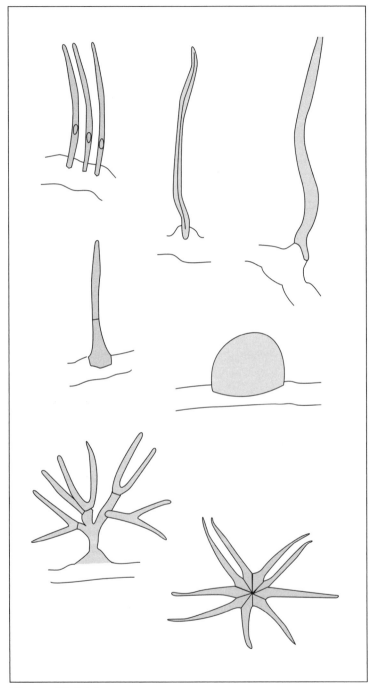

Figure 21 Trichomes

the land. Flames sometimes reached 9 to 13 meters (30 to 40 ft.) into the air.

Although frightening in their intensity and extent, prairie wildfires perform an important function in the grassland ecosystem. Prairie fires stimulate plant growth and keep the invading trees at bay.

Investigate the role of fire on the prairie without striking a match! You'll need black aquarium gravel or black sand (to simulate scorched earth), a shovel, a rake, measuring tape, eight stakes, string, a permanent marker, four laboratory thermometers, graph paper, and your journal. You can borrow the thermometers from your school science department, but select four that give the same reading at room temperature.

Begin this experiment in late winter. Locate a small area 1 × 3 meters (3 × 9 ft.) in your yard or in a nearby empty lot or field that receives full sunlight at least 6 hours a day and where grasses grow well. Be sure to obtain permission from the landowner if you will be working on someone else's property. Mark the corners with stakes and outline the area with string. Now divide the area into three equal squares using string and four additional stakes. Label the plots A, B, and C by marking the stake in the lower left corner of each plot.

Remove the sod from plots A and B using a shovel. Replace the lost layer with topsoil. Tamp the loosened dirt with your feet or hands. On plot B, scatter a thin layer of black sand or aquarium gravel to cover approximately half the total area. Leave plot C unaltered. Allow the grass to grow in this plot during the course of this experiment.

In your journal, draw a chart in which to record daily afternoon soil and air temperatures, in °C or °F, for each plot. To measure soil temperatures in plots A and B, scratch a thumb-size depression in the surface of the soil. Place the bulb of the thermometer in the hole. Be sure to keep the bulb of the thermometer out of the direct sun as you take a reading. Leave the thermometer in place for 15 minutes or until the reading stabilizes. Measure the soil temperature in plot C by placing the bulb at the base of the grasses, just underneath the dead thatch. At the same time, record the air

Prairie fires stimulate plant growth.

temperature. Record the information in your journal. Continue daily readings throughout the spring.

Graph your data for all three plots. Let the horizontal axis represent time in days, and the vertical axis, temperature in °C or °F. In which plot did the soil warm up the soonest? Can you explain why? How might warmer soil temperatures in the spring affect the timing of new plant growth?

In addition to affecting soil temperature, what other factor critical for plant growth is affected by fire? (Hint: Fire removes dead leaves and stems that shade the ground.)

✔ Doing More
Surf the Konza Prairie's Web site to watch a video of a prairie fire, at http://climate.konza.ksu.edu/general/news.html.

CHAPTER 5

The Give and Take of Prairie Life

TODAY'S PRAIRIE SEEMS LIKE SUCH A simple place. Grasses and wildflowers grow and blossom. Herbivores eat the plants while carnivores and omnivores prey on the plant-eaters. To most observers, these statements sum up the major relationships on a prairie. But the prairie ecosystem isn't as simple as it looks. Much of what goes on in a prairie is hidden from our eyes. Plants especially lead secret lives.

In the conflict between plants and plant-eaters, plants seem to be the losers. Unable to run from their attackers, how can they fight back? Some prairie plants grow hairs called trichomes on their leaves. The thick mat of hair keeps out small herbivores. On the shortgrass prairie, many forbs store noxious chemicals in their leaves to repel herbivores. Even grasses carry on their own secret chemical war against herbivores, with help from fungi that invade their roots.

85

Plants also fight amongst themselves—for space to grow, soil nutrients, and sunlight. Some prairie plants attack their neighbors with chemical warfare. Chemicals called **allelochemicals**, released from roots or leached from leaves, inhibit seed germination and growth of neighboring plants.

Even in matters of reproduction, plants are quite devious. With large, showy flowers loaded with sugary nectar and pollen, plants attract many small animals. As the animals travel from flower to flower, they unknowingly act as couriers, transferring reproductive cells and helping plants set seed.

Some prairie relationships never see the light of day. Deep in the soil, special bacteria take up residence in the roots of prairie peas. These bacteria, called **nitrogen-fixing bacteria**, convert nitrogen from the air into chemicals useful to the plant. The plant, in turn, creates the perfect home for the bacteria, in a structure called a **root nodule**.

The members of a prairie community are intricately bound to each other and to their environment in many

Table 12 Grassland Plants That Produce Allelochemicals	
Common Name	**Scientific Name**
Prairie sunflower	*Helianthus pauciflorus*
Western sunflower	*Helianthus occidentalis*
Common sunflower	*Helianthus annuus*
Prairie coreopsis	*Coreopsis palmata*
Pussy toes	*Antennaria palmata*
Culver's root	*Andropogon virginicum*
Broomsedge	*Andropogon virginicus*
Flowering spurge	*Euphorbia corollata*
Johnson grass	*Sorghum halepense*
Meadow fescue	*Festuca elatior*
Crabgrass	*Sigitaria sanguinalis*
Prairie threeawn	*Aristida oligantha*

strange and fascinating ways. Use the activities that follow to explore a few of these relationships.

But don't stop there! Include a visit to a prairie dog town, the hub of life on the plains. Prairie dogs make their homes underground, living in colonies or towns comprised of hundreds to thousands of individuals. Their town can also be home to many other creatures. A study of a black-tailed prairie dog town in South Dakota uncovered 134 species of vertebrates. What uninvited guests can you observe?

INVESTIGATION 5

Grassland Wars: A Look at How Plants Do Battle

Some grassland plants pack a chemical arsenal in their leaves and roots. A silent battle begins as the chemicals leak out from the roots and leaves and enter the surrounding soil.

Which plants engage in these silent battles? To find out, you'll need radish seeds, a kitchen or postal scale, a ruler, white paper towels, plastic sandwich bags, a pipette or tablespoon, distilled water, a stovetop, cheesecloth, a funnel, a pot, a graduated cylinder or measuring cup, several jars with lids, a marker, a long-shafted screwdriver, and your journal. Gather field guides that cover grasses, wildflowers, and weeds.

Select a few grasses or forbs from a nearby grassy field or natural grassland to test for the production of harmful chemicals. Be on the lookout for sunflowers, many of which are known to produce inhibitory substances. From each plant species you wish to test, collect enough leaves (or roots and rhizomes) to stuff a plastic sandwich bag. *Don't strip all the leaves from a single plant!* Keep the leaves or roots from the same species together. Label and date the bag. Use field guides to identify the plant or make a rough sketch in your journal for future reference. Refrigerate the samples as soon as you return from the field.

The first step in processing your samples is to leach the chemicals out of the plant using boiling water. The watery soup that's produced is called an extract. To make an extract, weigh out 28 grams (1 oz.) of leaves (or roots and rhizomes) from one plant species. Tear the plant into small pieces and place the pieces in a pot. Add 400 milliliters (2 cups) of water. Boil the mixture for 5 minutes. ***Be careful! Both the hot water and the steam rising from its surface can burn!***

Let the mixture cool. After it has cooled, set a funnel inside the opening of a small jar. Line the inside of the funnel with cheesecloth. Pour the cooled mixture into the funnel. Discard the shredded plant and label the jar containing the extract. Cap it and place the extract in the refrigerator while you finish making extracts of other plant samples.

Radish seeds germinate within 5 to 7 days and are sensitive to inhibitory chemicals. Before you test your extracts on germinating radish seeds, do a test run. This will allow you to observe how the seeds grow and develop normally. Fold a paper towel to fit inside a plastic sandwich bag. Add just enough distilled water to wet the towel, without leaving any excess water. Place 20 radish seeds on top of the towel and close the plastic bag. **Incubate** the seeds by storing the bag at room temperature in a dark place for 7 days. Examine the bag at the end of the incubation period.

Once you know how long it takes for radish seedlings to grow, test each extract. Using a separate plastic bag for each extract sample, add enough extract to wet a folded paper towel placed inside a sandwich bag. Add 20 radish seeds, label the bags, and incubate them. At the same time, run a control that consists of a sandwich bag with 20 seeds, paper towel, and water—but no extract. After the incubation period, examine the seedlings in each bag. Measure the length of each shoot. Record the data in your journal.

To analyze your data, determine the average shoot length for the seedlings in each plastic bag. Add the lengths of the shoots and divide that value by the number of seedlings measured. Which extracts appeared to inhibit radish germination?

Living Together: A Study of Symbiosis in the Pea Family

While competition is a common theme in a grassland, some relationships, such as the **symbiotic** relationship between nitrogen-fixing bacteria and plants of the pea family, are quite cozy.

You can check out this unusual partnership right at home. Collect potting soil, several large pots, pea, alfalfa, or clover seeds, inoculant (solution containing nitrogen-fixing bacteria), a marker, a soft drink, paper towels, a dissection kit, microscope slides, cover slips, a compound microscope, a hand lens, a ruler, toothpicks, a medicine dropper, an alcohol lamp, methylene blue stain, a hand trowel, and your journal. Visit a farm supply store to pick up the seeds and inoculant. If the store doesn't have what you need, order from a biological supply house or nursery (see Appendix). Borrow the dissection kit, microscope, slides, cover slips, and stain from your school science department.

Soak the seeds in wet paper towels overnight. The next day, fill four pots with potting soil. Label two pots as "treated" and two pots "untreated." Now collect half of the seeds in a small container. Add enough soft drink to coat the seeds, then add the inoculant following the manufacturer's directions. Sprinkle the treated seeds over the soil in the pots labeled "treated." Plant the untreated seeds in the other pots. Cover the seeds with a thin layer of potting soil, pat it down with your hands, and set the pots near a sunny window or outside in warm weather. Water them daily.

When the plants are 8 to 10 weeks old, dig up a few from each pot. Wash the roots. Examine them closely for root nodules. You will find these small growths up and down the main root as well as along smaller roots of the treated plants. What do they look like with a hand lens? Carefully cut one open with a scalpel. Record your observations.

To observe the bacteria inside the root nodules, crush a cut nodule between two microscope slides. Remove the top slide and the nodule. Next place a drop of water on the smear left by the nodule. Let the slide dry. Pass it over a flame a few times. After it has cooled, flood the slide with methylene blue for 2 minutes. Rinse with water. View it under high power using a compound microscope. The bacteria will appear as small, dark-stained bodies shaped like short dashes.

A Community of Diners: Insect Diversity on a Single Plant

Wildflowers offer a diverse menu to their animal visitors. Herbivores can feed on leaves, stems, sap, roots, and flowers, including pollen, nectar, petals, and seeds. Predators pick and choose among the many plant-eaters. On some wildflowers, you might find 400 or more diners!

To observe such a dining extravaganza, check out several milkweed or goldenrod plants. Gather a field guide to wildflowers, a field guide to insects and spiders, a butterfly net, an insect sweep net, collecting jars, a pooter, a hand lens, tweezers, and your journal. A pooter is a device used to collect tiny insects. You can find directions for making your own in the Appendix.

Both milkweed and goldenrod can be found along roadsides and in fields, meadows, and prairies. Look for these plants in the summer or fall. Use a field guide to help you recognize them.

Once you have located a patch of goldenrod or milkweed, pick a warm, sunny day to study their dining community. Approach the plants slowly and remain at arm's length, for some of the insects may sense danger and escape by flying away or simply dropping to the ground.

Scan the plant from top to bottom. Look along the stem, on the upper and lower leaf surfaces, and on the flower heads. Some creatures will be well camouflaged or hidden, so search carefully.

Table 13   The Milkweed Community

Herbivores

Leaf eaters: monarch caterpillars, queen caterpillars
Nectar drinkers: bumblebees, honey bees, monarch, queen,
   and haristreak butterflies, ants, wasps, hawk or sphinx moth,
   gemeter moth, underwing moth
Sap sippers: aphids
Pollen eaters: bees
Stem eaters: larvae of milkweed beetles
Root eaters: larvae of milkweed beetles
Seed eaters: large milkweed bugs, small milkweed bugs

Predators

Spiders: crab spiders
Insects: yellow jackets, hairy black tachnid fly

Table 14   The Goldenrod Community

Herbivores

Leaf eaters: leafhoppers, goldenrod beetles
Nectar drinkers: honey bees, carpenter bees, bumblebees,
   wasps, hover flies, syrphid flies, moths, butterflies
Flower eaters: Japanese beetle
Sap sippers: bugs, aphids, hoppers, lacewings
Pollen eaters: longhorn beetles (such as adult locust borer),
   soldier beetle, blister beetle, paper wasp, bees
Stem eaters: small fly larvae (ball gall), gelechiid moth larvae
   (elliptical gall), midge (ball gall)
Root eaters: nematodes

Predators

Spiders: harvestmen (dadylonglegs), garden spiders, crab
   spiders
Insects: assassin bug, ambush bug, praying mantis

How many different types of insects or spiders do you
see? Which seem to be the most abundant? Make a chart
to record your tally. Consult a field guide to help you identify
the creatures. If you need to, use a pooter, an insect sweep
net, or a butterfly net to capture a specimen for a closer look.

If you still can't identify the animal, collect a sample specimen to examine at home.

After you've completed the survey, take a closer, longer look at the behavior of each animal. How many appear to be feeding? How many are simply resting? What other types of activities can you observe? Which plant part attracts the most visitors?

The Comings and Goings of Flower Visitors

Advertising pays, even in the natural world. Look at any wild-flower on a warm, sunny day. With bright, showy petals and enticing scents, wildflowers lure animal visitors. Promising sweet nectar in return for a small favor, wildflowers offer land-ing platforms and guide strips to help their visitors find their way. Unknowingly, the animal visitor delivers pollen grains con-taining male sex cells to nearby flowers as it searches for more nectar.

How well does a flower's advertising pay off? To begin to answer this question, you'll need the following equipment. Gather a hand lens, a stop watch, a field guide to wildflowers, a field guide to insects, an insect sweep net, a butterfly net, cotton balls, ethyl acetate, collecting jars, and your journal. Purchase ethyl acetate from a pharmacist or biological sup-ply company. ***Ethyl acetate is a flammable liquid. Keep it away from any heat source or open flame.***

On a warm, sunny day, visit a prairie or grassy field with lots of wildflowers in bloom. Locate a cluster of blossoms on plants of the same species. Use a field guide to identify the plant, then take a moment to study the structure of the flower with your hand lens. Can you locate the anthers and stigma (see Project 1)? Dust some of the pollen into your hand. Now look inside the flower along the petals, sepals, ovary, and sta-mens, for structures that look like small blisters. These are the **nectaries**.

Table 15　Flower Visitation Observation Sheet

Directions: Under "Notes," use abbreviations to record the following information for each insect visitor at 5-minute intervals: activities while on the plant, including resting (R), grooming (G), mating (M), laying eggs (Eg), eating or collecting pollen (P), drinking nectar (N).

Plant: _____

Observer: _____　　Common name: _____

Date: _____　　Scientific name: _____

Time: _____

Weather conditions: _____　　Description (plant height, number of blooms, flower color, type): _____

Visitor Number	Visitor Name	Time	Length of Visit	Notes
1				
2				
3				

Imagine that you are a bumblebee. What path would you take to reach the nectaries, once you've landed? Do you brush against the anthers, getting dusted with pollen, on the way?

Now that you've analyzed the flower design, you're ready to watch the show! Find a comfortable spot from which to observe the flowers without disturbing the insect visitors. First just sit back and watch the comings and goings of a few visitors. What does each insect do once it has landed? If it is feeding, can you tell what it's eating?

Now begin recording your observations. Initially categorize each visitor as a butterfly, moth, fly, beetle, bee, bat, or hummingbird, until you have a chance to thumb through your field guide. Spend an hour at different times of the day observing the visitors. Include an hour of observation around dusk. At 5-minute intervals during the hour, record each visitor's activity. Which insects seem to be frequent visitors? How many guests came by in a 1-hour period? Which visitors come by only in the morning? Which prefer the evening?

✔ Doing More

To find out who's carrying pollen, nab a visitor with a net just as it is about to leave the flower. With your hand lens, examine its body closely for pollen grains. If you have caught a bee or wasp, add a wad of cotton that has been soaked with ethyl acetate to the net. Once the insect appears anesthetized, transfer it quickly to a collecting jar to examine.

To track an insect from one flower to the next, try marking it with a dot of nail polish or correcting fluid. Make an insect holder using the directions given in the Appendix. Use the holder to restrain the insect while you mark it.

PROJECT **21**

Ants, Aphids, and Honey-Dew

Ants have a great fondness for a sweetened drink called honey-dew. It doesn't come in a can or bottle. You won't find it at the grocery store or quick stop. This sugary liquid drips out the back end of small, pear-shaped insects called aphids. Aphids suck on the sap of plants, excreting the excess fluid. By stroking the aphids with their antennae, ants can stimulate the aphids to produce this drink almost on demand.

Would you like to watch this strange relationship up close? Collect a small ant farm no larger than 30 centimeters (12 in.) long and 25 centimeters (10 in.) tall with a connecting port; ants; a 37.9-liter (10-gal.) aquarium; 60 centimeters (24 in.) of 1- or 1.2-centimeter (0.3937- to 0.4724-in.) plastic tubing; masking tape; a white plastic spoon; tweezers; a small sponge; a hand lens; a white sheet; collecting jars; work gloves; a shovel; scissors; cardboard; a plant infected with aphids; a small vase or jar; a window screening; and your journal.

You can purchase an ant farm at some toy stores, pet shops, museum gift shops, or from a biological supplier (see Appendix for addresses). Follow the manufacturer's directions to set it up. Buy plastic tubing from a pet supplier that carries fish and aquarium products, or a home building supply store.

Where can you get the ants? In many cases, if you've bought an ant farm, you'll receive information on ordering ants. But, if you want to collect your own, follow the directions given below. Just be sure your ant farm is set up and ready for occupancy before your ants arrive!

Gather a white sheet, collecting jar, plastic spoon, and shovel to collect your own ants. Search your yard, a nearby field, or a vacant lot for ants. Look for mounds of freshly dug dirt. *If you live in the southeastern United States, beware of fire ants! These ants deliver a nasty bite. Avoid any red ants around a large mound over 15 to 20 centimeters (6 to 8 in.) tall.* Turn over any stones and follow any ants that you find. Eventually they will lead you to a nest, which may be above or below ground.

Near the nest, spread a sheet on the ground. Put on work gloves to protect your hands from biting ants. With a shovel, carefully dig into the soil at the nest site. Transfer the soil to the sheet. Sort through the dirt to find adults, pupae, and larvae. Larvae will appear oblong, white, and shiny, while pupae live in white cocoons with a parchment-like exterior. Spoon the ants into a collecting jar. Continue digging carefully (dig deep!) and sifting through the dirt to find an ant much larger than the others. This will be the queen. By including the queen in your ant farm, you'll be able to observe many generations of ants. Without her, the captive colony will live just a short time.

Back at home, place the ants in the refrigerator for a hour to slow them down. Working quickly, use a spoon to transfer the ants to the ant farm. Add a small piece of moistened sponge in one corner. Close the port securely when you are through. Place the ant farm in a dark room or closet.

The next day, after the ants have settled in, introduce small bits of fruit, vegetable, oatmeal, or bread. Find out what the ants like best. Replace old food with fresh using tweezers. Add a few drops of water daily to keep the sponge moist.

Once or twice a day, take out the ant farm to observe the ants. Use a hand lens to watch them build tunnels, groom themselves, and eat.

To watch ants drink honey-dew, locate a colony of aphids. Aphids attack the leaves and stems of all sorts of plants, from rose bushes to trees, weeds, and wildflowers. These tiny sapsuckers come in many shades, most often yellow, green, red, brown, or black. Consult any gardener, for they will undoubtedly know these common pests!

When you've found a plant with aphids, take a few cuttings of the infested area. Place the cuttings in a vase or jar with water, then put it in a corner of the aquarium. Cut out a small cardboard collar to cover the opening of the vase or jar. Now introduce the ant farm into the aquarium. Cut a piece of tubing just long enough to connect the connecting port of the ant farm to the plant cuttings. Use tape to secure both ends of the tubing. The end leading to the plant cuttings should rest on top of the cardboard collar. Cover the aquarium with a window screen. Set the aquarium near a window but away from direct sunlight.

The ants will use the tubing as a trail. How long did it take them to find the aphids? Use a hand lens to watch the behavior of the ants. How did the aphids react to the ants?

✔ Doing More

Ladybird beetles, or ladybugs, naturally prey on aphids. Watch what happens when you introduce these beetles to your ant/aphid terrarium. Collect ladybugs or order them from a local garden shop or nursery.

Observe other insect species interactions on plants in your yard or a neighboring field.

CHAPTER 6

Saving America's Grasslands

WHAT WOULD IT HAVE BEEN LIKE, LIVing on the prairie in the mid 1800's? You might have lived on a farm far from neighbors or town. Your father worked hard to guide his oxen and plow through the tough prairie sod. Your mother grew a small vegetable garden. Although she missed the trees back home, she loved the prairie flowers. She kept a small prairie garden on the side of the house. Beyond the farm, the prairie extended as far as you could see. You loved hiding in the tall prairie grasses or laying on your back staring at imaginary figures in the clouds. With your brother and sister, you chased prairie chickens and whistled to the cheery meadowlarks.

A lot has changed in the last 150 years! Less than 1% of the original tallgrass prairie still stands and much of the western prairie has changed. What do you think happened to the prairie?

Settlers continued to move onto the prairie. They plowed the land and broke up the sod. Corn and wheat now grow in place of big bluestem, switchgrass, and Indian grass. The plow and the wind have removed much of the fertile topsoil. Too many cattle grazed on the western prairie. Instead of prairie grasses and wildflowers, millions of planted trees and other exotic plants grow in the prairie soil.

The animals, too, have changed. Once tens of millions of American bison walked the prairie, pursued by packs of wolves and occasional Plains grizzlies and hunted by Native Americans for food and clothing. With the arrival of white hunters, the bison were rapidly slaughtered for sport, their hides, and their tongues. The train tracks also divided herds, because bison would not cross them. Ranchers and settlers drove the gray wolf north into Canada. The prairie dog, long despised by ranchers, has been poisoned, shot, and even gassed out of its tunnels. Fewer waterfowl fly the famous prairie migratory pathways in the spring and fall. Even prairie birds like the bobolink and meadowlark have declined because of habitat loss.

The settlers did more than just plow the prairie. They brought with them plants and animals from their part of the world. These exotic or nonnative species sometimes displaced the natives. Birds, such as the English sparrow or starlings, compete with native grassland birds for food and nest cavities. Plants, such as leafy spurge, purple loosestrife, and spotted knapweed, have aggressively taken over thousands to millions of acres of native prairie.

Early prairie settlers also put out prairie fires. Fire plays an important role in this ecosystem. Without fire, trees and shrubs invade the prairie. Dead leaves and stems gather, blocking the light to plants below.

With all these changes, is there any hope for the prairie that remains? What can you do to help? The activities in this chapter will help you answer these questions.

Preserving Grassland Birds

What's happening to our grassland birds? Today, less than half as many grasshopper sparrows live on our grasslands than were found there 25 years ago. The bobolink, upland sparrow, and other birds of prairies and fields are also in trouble.

What can you do to help? By pinpointing active nests in fields and alerting landowners and farmers, you can do a lot! You'll need a pair of binoculars, field guides to birds and nests (see Appendix for listing), stakes, flagging or strips of fabric, a tape measure, and your journal.

In the fall, find a grassy field, hayfield, or prairie. Because most birds that breed in grasslands require 5 to 200 acres or more, look for large areas. Be sure to obtain landowner permission before you begin your study.

First do a preliminary survey of the site before any fall or winter mowing. The now-abandoned nests should be easier to spot among the dried grasses. Sketch out a rough map in your journal. Using steady, regular steps or paces, walk a straight line along one boundary of the field. Count your paces as you walk. This will help you map any nests that you find.

Look for nests hidden in the dense stalks of grasses or shrubs. Some nests may sit on the ground, while others may be woven among a cluster of grass or wildflower stems or tucked in the branches of a shrub. A few birds will even make a nest on a patch of bare dirt (see Table 16 for a description of nests of common grassland birds). When you find a nest, place a stake in the ground to mark the site. Record the location in your journal, noting the number of paces from where you began counting.

Continue pacing along a straight line, until you reach the end of the field. Turn and walk five paces, then turn again to walk back down the field. Count your paces as you search carefully for nests. Survey as much of the area as you can using this procedure.

In the spring, birds will begin to migrate back into the

Table 16 Nest Description of Common Grassland Birds

Bobolink

Cup nest in depression on ground at base of dense cover of forbs in mat of dead grass 1 meter (3.3 ft.) or less in height

Eastern meadowlark

Well-concealed domed cup nest, often with a runway, in depression on ground in dens cover with vegetation 0.25 to 0.5 meter (10 to 20 in.) tall

Savannah sparrow

Cup nest in shallow depression on ground, formed in grass clumps or at base of low woddy shrub

Grasshopper sparrow

Cup nest in depression on ground under clump of overhanging litter and grasses or at base of shrub, mostly domed

Vesper sparrow

Cup nest in depression on ground concealed by sparse vegetation at base of forb or thin clump of grass

Upland sandpdper

Shallow depression on dry habitat concealed with grass

Killdeer

Shallow depression on open ground, in dirt or gravel

Eastern meadowlark nest

Grasshopper sparrow nest

Killdeer nest

Vesper sparrow nest

Table 17   Management Practices to Conserve Grassland Birds[1]

1. Avoid mowing until after August 1 to allow breeding pairs to raise one to two broods.
   OR
   Give wide clearance to known nesting sites when mowing.

2. Use a flushing bar when mowing.

3. Avoid night mowing.

4. Raise mowing blade to 15 cm (6 in.) height.

5. Limit mowing to every 1 to 3 years for any given field.

6. Reserve fields not useful for hay production for wildlife.

7. Convert rescue fields or fields with other nonnative grasses and wildflower to native grasses and wildflowers.

8. If multiple fields are to be converted, try to save adjacent or contiguous lands.

9. Avoid overgrazing pastures. Keep cattle off field between June 1 and July 15.

[1]Taken from *Conserving Grassland Birds, Vol. I, II, and III*, by Andrea Jones and Peter Vickerey, Massachusetts Audubon Society, 1985.

grassland. By May, you may see new nests being built. Check staked sites from last year's nests first, to see if they're being used again. Complete a second survey to detect any new nests. *Approach nests cautiously. Use binoculars to observe the birds. Many nesting pairs are easily disturbed and may abandon a nest!* Mark current nests on your map.

When you have mapped the nests, alert the landowner or farmer who may be contracted to mow the field. By influencing their mowing or grazing practices, you'll help ensure that these birds successfully raise their broods. Plan a meeting with the landowner or farmer. Bring along an adult, information on the nesting birds, and a copy of suggested management practices (see Table 17). Be polite and friendly.

Continue monitoring the breeding birds. How many chicks

did each pair raise successfully? Which pairs raised more than one brood in the season? What do you think contributes to good nesting success?

Planting a Prairie Garden

Surprise your family with a beautiful bed of attractive grasses and showy wildflowers that blossom from June through September. Plant a prairie garden. The garden will attract birds and butterflies and, after the first year, will be almost maintenance free.

You'll need sun-loving wildflowers and grasses native to your area, a shovel, a tiller, clean straw, bags of topsoil, 7.5-meter (25-ft.) measuring tape, string, stakes, a garden hose, and your journal. Write or phone prairie nurseries for their catalogs (see Appendix for addresses and phone numbers). Contact the nearest botanical garden to obtain lists of prairie or grassland plants native to your area. Don't forget to ask your parent's permission to dig up a part of the yard.

Long before you put a spade or plant in the ground, you should consider where to place the garden, what plants to buy, when to plant, and how to arrange the plants.

Look for a sunny spot that receives at least 6 to 8 hours of full sun daily. Start with a garden plot that is 3×3 meters (or 10×10 ft.) or smaller.

To select plants that will grow well in your garden, examine the soils and moisture level in your plot. Record your findings in your journal. As you look through catalogs or visit a local nursery, cross off those plant species not suited to the soils in your garden plot. Begin a list of plants you'd like to include.

How do you want to arrange the plants? Use the following principles to guide you. Then make a sketch of what you want your garden to look like.

- In a plot that backs up to a wall or fence, place shorter plants in front and taller plants in back. In circular plots without a backdrop, place taller plants in the center with shorter plants in outlying areas.
- Plant groupings of one type of wildflower, not just one plant.
- Fill in areas between flower groups with grasses.
- Use mostly shorter plants for smaller garden plots and taller plants for larger areas.
- Space plants about 30 centimeters (12 in.) apart.

In the early spring, outline your plot with stakes and string. Remove the top 7 centimeters (3 in.) of grass and soil. Rent a sod-cutter to do this or use a shovel and tiller. Fill in the area with topsoil. To kill any weeds that may pop up later, till the soil three times at 1-week intervals.

Have your plants in hand by late spring. If you order through the mail, place the order in plenty of time. Mark a grid of planting sites in your prepared soil bed, using the tape measure and stakes. Once all the sites are marked, begin planting, starting at one end of the garden. Follow any special planting directions from your nursery or mail-order company. Mulch with about 7 centimeters (3 in.) of clean (weed-free) straw, then water thoroughly. Water daily until you see signs of new growth.

Once your garden is in the ground, you can begin to enjoy its beauty. Be on guard for any weeds that pop up during the first year or two. Pull up weeds as soon as you see them. Water only if a severe dry spell sets in during the first growing season.

In the spring of the second year, mow down last year's growth with a lawn mower. Rake thoroughly to remove the dead stems and leaves. Each spring in following years, mow and rake at least half of the garden. Leave the other half standing, as it may contain cocoons and **over-wintering** insect eggs.

Seed Savers:
Preserving the Next Generation

Like treasure hunters, prairie seed collectors search high and low for native prairie plants. They scan along back roads, railroad beds, steep hillsides, and unplowed land too poor to farm. By saving native seeds, they help preserve the future.

You, too, can learn to collect seeds of native plants. Use these seeds to plant a prairie garden or restore a prairie patch (see Projects 23 and 26). You'll need a field guide to grasses and wildflowers (see Appendix), pruning shears, sheets of newspaper, a permanent marker, a rolling pin, work gloves, a dust mask, safety glasses, seed storage containers (small glass or plastic jars, paper envelopes, film canisters), paper bags, seed cleaning screens with frames (see Appendix), strips of fabric, and your journal.

In the summer or early fall, locate a few native plants that you would like to include in your prairie or prairie garden. Use a field guide to identify the plants. Flag each plant so that you can easily locate it later. If the plants are on public lands, you may need a permit to collect seeds. If the land is privately owned, seek permission from the landowner. Return to the site every few days to monitor the plant's growth and development. Once the plant has begun flowering, watch it closely for development of seeds.

How will you know when the seeds are ripe? The petals will fade, wither, and fall to the ground, leaving behind a seed head, pod, follicle, fruit, or other seed-bearing container. Look for changes in the color of the seed receptacle. When ripe, seeds may rattle in their pods or fall easily from a seed head. Run your hand up the seed head to check for release of seeds. Ripe seeds are plump, hard, and usually brown or black, while unripe seeds are usually soft and green.

Collect on a sunny day after any dew or raindrops have evaporated. Bring along pruning shears, a permanent marker, work gloves, several paper bags, and your journal.

Collect seeds by clipping the plant stem well below the seed head. Keep each plant species separate. Record the date, location, time of collection, and species name in your journal. *Never harvest more than half of the seed from any plant!*

At home, set a seed screen with a coarse meshing on a table with the mesh side up. Place a full sheet of newspaper under the seed screen. Rake the seed heads across the screen to release the seeds. The seeds will fall to the newspaper below, along with some plant debris. Winnow out any plant debris by pouring the mixture from cup to cup while blowing or standing in front of a breezy open window or fan. Be sure to wear a dust mask and safety glasses.

Some seed heads such as those of the coneflower and black-eyed Susan can be very tough. They don't break apart easily. Try crushing them apart with a rolling pin. Work the rolling pin on top of a sheet of newspaper to collect the broken heads and seeds. Winnow the debris from the seeds using a fan or wind.

Dry your seeds to protect them from fungi or moisture. Spread cleaned seeds on a few sheets of newspaper in an out-of-the way place. Let them sit for two weeks. Remember to label each newspaper spread! After all seeds have dried, put them in dry glass or plastic containers. If you prefer envelopes, be sure to place the envelopes in a rodent-free container. Store them in a cool, dry room until you are ready to plant.

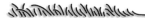

The Aliens Have Landed: Native Versus Nonnative Plants

Many of them came across the ocean as stowaways, hidden as tiny seeds in straw or hay, bags of cereals and grains, or in the soil used as ballast on a ship. In less than 200 years after landing on our shores, these tiny aliens spread across our country, traveling down railroad lines, across wagon trails, in soil clinging to the hooves of horses, oxen, or cattle, or even to the boots and shoes of westward pioneers. Today approximately 20% to 33% of all plant species in North America came from other places.

Some of these aliens might look quite natural to us, but in many cases, native wildlife finds them useless for cover, food, or shelter. Some even cause sickness when eaten. The more aggressive aliens outcompete the native plants for available resources, and in some cases have totally taken over hundreds of millions of acres of land.

Just who are these aliens? Where can they be found? They are everywhere. Just outside your front door you're likely to be greeted by an entire lawn of alien plants, for most lawn grasses have been imported from Africa or Asia. You'll also find nonnatives growing along the roadsides, in empty lots, abandoned farm fields, pastures, hay meadows, and prairies.

All you need to find these nonnative plants is a hand lens, sturdy walking shoes, a sampling frame, stakes and strips of fabric or flagging, a few friends, your journal, and a field guide to weeds (see Appendix).

First select an area to survey for nonnative plants. Get to know the plants that live there. Use your field guide to determine which are native and which are not. Keep a list in your journal.

Once you're familiar with most of the plants, use a sampling frame to determine the percentage of nonnatives. Directions for making a frame are included in the Appendix. Stake off a rectangular area 3 × 20 meters (10 × 66 ft.) that runs through a representative section of the field. Within this rectangle, randomly select 20 plots to sample with the sampling frame.

Within each sampling plot, count and identify all stems. Record the species name and country or region of origin in your journal. Determine the percentage of nonnative stems by adding the total number of nonnative stems and dividing by the total number of stems (native plus nonnative). Continue surveying the remaining sampling plots. Average the percentages by adding them and dividing by 20 or the number of plots analyzed.

To learn which aliens are the most damaging in your area, contact your local county extension service or your state's department of conservation. You can usually find their phone numbers in a special section of your phone book called the blue pages. Under the U.S. Government listings, look for the Department of Agriculture, Agricultural Extension Service. What is being done to control these weedy invaders?

PROJECT **26**

Restoring a Patch of Prairie

Across the Midwest, a growing number of prairie enthusiasts are working hard to bring the prairie back. They are restoring badly damaged prairies and converting old farmlands to prairie lands.

If you live in a prairie state, you, too, can plant a prairie. Make it a neighborhood or school project. Talk to your friends, classmates, teachers, and parents. You'll need plenty of helpers and enough money to purchase seeds (about $500 for $\frac{1}{4}$ acre)! Borrow a tiller or tractor with a tiller, a disc, or a harrow, a garden rake, and string trimmer (Weed-eater is one trade name) or lawnmower with adjustable mowing height. To obtain seeds, write or call for catalogs from nurseries that specialize in native grasses and wildflowers (see Appendix for a listing). Gather a tape measure (minimum length of 7.5 meters or 25 ft.), a hand trowel, several bags of peat moss or vermiculite, a clean kitchen garbage can or large bucket, and mulch—clean, weed-free straw (not field hay), to spread over the newly sown seeds. An outside hose bib and a length of garden hose long enough to reach the plot may be needed during a dry spell.

First prepare the ground. By tilling the soil several times at weekly or biweekly intervals before planting seeds, you can greatly reduce the competing weeds and ensure a greater germination rate of the prairie seeds. If you are converting a lawn, first remove the top 7 centimeters (3 in.) of grass and dirt using a shovel or sod-cutter (these can be rented). Till the bed to a depth of 10 to 13 centimeters (4 to 5 in.) three times over a period of 3 to 6 weeks. Then, rake the bed to level it prior to seeding. Avoid old weedy fields unless you are willing to work the plot biweekly from spring to fall to get rid of long-lived weedy plants.

Meanwhile, in between tilling, search the catalogs for seeds or seed mixes. To know how much seed to purchase, you'll need to measure the area of the plot and analyze the soil. Measure the length and width in meters (or feet). Calculate the area by multiplying the length times the width. Lastly, decide if you want to plant a shortgrass prairie or a tallgrass prairie.

When you contact a nursery to place your order, ask for advice on the type of seed mix and amount of seed you'll need. Purchase as much seed as you can afford. You may be able to seed at a lower rate than recommended and still obtain good results. Plan to plant in late spring. Have the seeds shipped just in time for planting.

When you are ready to plant, fill a garbage can with 35 liters (8 gal.) of moist carrier—peat moss or vermiculite—for every 100 square meters (1,000 square ft.) of area that you are seeding. Stir a portion of seed mix into the garbage can at the rate recommended. Make sure the seeds and carrier are evenly mixed. Broadcast half of the mixture over the entire seedbed by grabbing a handful and flinging the mix in a wide arc. Walk a few steps farther and repeat the procedure until you have evenly covered the area. Now go back over the seedbed a second time, walking a path perpendicular to your first pass. Spread the remaining half of seed and carrier across the bed. Rake the seedbed to lightly cover the seed with 1 to 2 centimeters (0.4 to 0.8 in.) of soil, then firm the ground by walking across it with plenty of friends! Spread a thin cover of straw over the sown bed to hold in moisture. Water lightly in the early morning during the first 4 to 6 weeks. After that time, water only during a prolonged dry spell.

During the first growing season, fight weed growth by using a string trimmer or mower with a cutting height of 15 centimeters (6 in.). Prairie plants will grow slowly during the first year, spending most of their energies developing deep root systems. Most will not reach a height of 15 centimeters (6 in.) that first year. Weeds, however, grow much faster. Mow frequently enough to keep the weeds less than 30 centimeters (12 in.) in height.

In the spring of the second season, mow the prairie and rake off the cuttings. Keep an eye out for weeds and pull any that you see.

By the end of the second growing season, your prairie should be just starting to take over. Advertise it! Put up signs identifying the major wildflowers and grasses. Set up benches and walkways. Make it part of your community.

Conclusion

THE NORTH AMERICAN PRAIRIE IS A special place. Did you once think of it as flat and grassy? Hopefully, through the projects and investigations included here, you see the prairie a little differently! The "sea of grass" is actually a dynamic ecosystem where plants, animals, and microscopic creatures interact in many ways, sometimes competing, sometimes cooperating, or sometimes simply coexisting. Other elements such as fire, climate, weather, and earth help shape this complex web of life.

But what good is the prairie? Is it worth preserving? Yes! The North American prairie represents a unique American ecosystem. The beauty of the prairie lies in its wide-open spaces, rolling landscape, abundant light, and the colors and textures of its grasses and wildflowers. From April to September, the prairie treats its visitors to a magnificent display of wildflower blossoms. In the fall, the grasses show their colors, as their stems and leaves turn gold, rust, and wine-red. Some of the prairie's plant and animal life exist nowhere else in the world. The soils of the prairie are the envy of every farmer the world over. Soil scientists are still studying the process by which the prairie creates such rich earth. The prairie is also part of our cultural heritage, a symbol of the American frontier.

All across the country, groups of prairie enthusiasts are working hard to bring back the prairie. By saving native prairie seeds, clearing the land of nonnative forbs and trees, and planting native grasses and forbs, these people are restoring or recreating the prairie. As the grasses and forbs take over, native animals species also begin to return.

It's hard work to plant a prairie! Get involved. Put what you've learned about grasslands to good use. Help bring back the prairie. If you live in the prairie region, find out if any prairie conservation groups exist in your area. If you live outside the prairie states, support national groups, such as The Nature Conservancy, that are working to preserve America's prairies.

We'll never see what those early settlers to the prairie saw, or feel what they felt as they looked out over a wild land so different from what they left behind. But, perhaps one day, you may walk across a prairie where the grasses wave in the wind and wildflowers blossom, herds of bison graze, wolves howl in the distance, meadowlarks sing out their mating songs, and not a single house, farm, or factory can be seen in any direction.

Tools and Equipment

Basic Tools

Are you ready to go on a grassland safari? Although you can learn a lot just by using your eyes, nose, and ears, consider taking along the following pieces of equipment. They'll help reveal the hidden world of a field or prairie.

- binoculars
- a hand lens
- a long-shafted screwdriver
- a garden trowel
- a 15-centimeter (6-in.) ruler and 7.5-meter (25-ft.) tape measure
- collecting jars, plastic sandwich bags, and garbage bags
- tweezers (include a blunt pair and a pair with an extra-fine tip)
- surveyor's flagging or strips of fabric (bright colors only)
- small paper envelopes and glassine envelopes used by stamp collectors
- an aquarium net
- pruning shears or scissors

The following equipment can be made from materials that you may already have at home or can readily find at a hardware store or building supply store. Add these pieces to your bag of tricks!

Other Useful Equipment:

Butterfly Net

Butterflies are beautiful but elusive creatures. Have you ever tried to steal a closer look at one, only to have it fly off just when you reach it? Use a net! Once you're through, you can release the butterfly unharmed.

To make your own net, gather the following materials: 120 centimeters (4 ft.) of $\frac{3}{4}$ or 1-inch wooden doweling; a strip of canvas measuring 13 × 122 centimeters (5 × 48 in.); 156 centimeters (5 ft.) of 9-gauge wire; $1\frac{1}{2}$ yards of a sheer curtain fabric with a mesh size of 1 to 3 millimeters (0.04 to 0.12 in.); a meter stick or yard stick; two stainless-steel hose clamps ($\frac{9}{16}$ to $1\frac{1}{4}$ -in.); a sewing machine or needle and thread; an iron and ironing board; scissors; straight pins; a measuring tape; a sheet of newsprint or a roll of kraft paper at least 86 × 61 centimeters (34 × 24 in.); a marker; utility knife; pliers; a hammer; a screwdriver; and a drill and $\frac{7}{32}$ -inch drill bit. Purchase the fabric from a fabric store and hose clamps from a hardware or auto-parts store. An old mop handle or broom handle can be used in place of the wooden dowel.

To make the frame of the net, determine the exact center of the length of wire. Mark this point. Bend the wire at the indicated points (see figure 22). Work on a flat surface and use pliers to make the bends. Clip the free ends of the wire 1.5 centimeters ($\frac{1}{2}$ in.) from the last bend. With your hands, round the wire while bringing the two cut ends together to form a circle.

The net is cut from a pattern that you make yourself. Cut an 86 × 61-centimeter (34 × 24-in.) rectangle out of a sheet of paper. Fold the paper in half lengthwise. Using the figure on page 117 to guide you, redraw the pattern onto your sheet of paper. Use a ruler to draw any straight lines and freehand any arcs shown. Cut out the pattern from the sheet of paper.

Open up the pattern and lay it on top of the fabric so that a long edge of the pattern lines up against the fabric's fold (see figure 23). Pin the pattern to the fabric, placing pins every 5 centimeters (2 in.) close to the edge of the pattern. Cut the fabric along the pattern's edge. Remove the pattern and pins. With a sewing machine or needle and thread, stitch along the cut fabric edges about 1 centimeter ($\frac{1}{2}$ in.) in from the edge. Begin at a corner at the mouth of the net and sew towards the cone and back to the other corner of the mouth. Don't sew the mouth of the net closed! Turn the sewn fabric inside out to form a long, cone-shaped net.

To attach the net to the metal frame, fold the edges of the canvas strip 1 centimeter ($\frac{1}{2}$ in.) under and press with an iron. Now fold the fabric in half lengthwise and press again. Drape the strip over the frame along the pressed fold. Sandwich the cut edge of the net's opening between the two pieces of canvas. Using a needle and thread, sew the canvas strip to the net.

Prepare the handle by drilling a 5-millimeter ($\frac{7}{32}$ -in.) diameter hole 9 centimeters ($3\frac{1}{2}$ in.) from one end of the dowel. Rotate the dowel 180 degrees and drill a second hold 6.5 centimeters ($2\frac{1}{2}$ in.) from the same end of the dowel. With a utility knife, cut two shallow, V-shaped grooves from each hole to the end of the rod. The grooves should be just deep enough to snugly fit the wire you used for framing. Fit the shaped net frame to the handle and drive the wire ends into the drilled openings with a hammer.

To secure the net frame to the doweling, slide two hose clamps over the handle as shown in the figure. Use a screwdriver to tighten the hose clamps.

Practice using your net so that you won't harm any butterfly that you catch. If you spot a butterfly in flight, slowly follow it and watch where it lands. If it lands on a

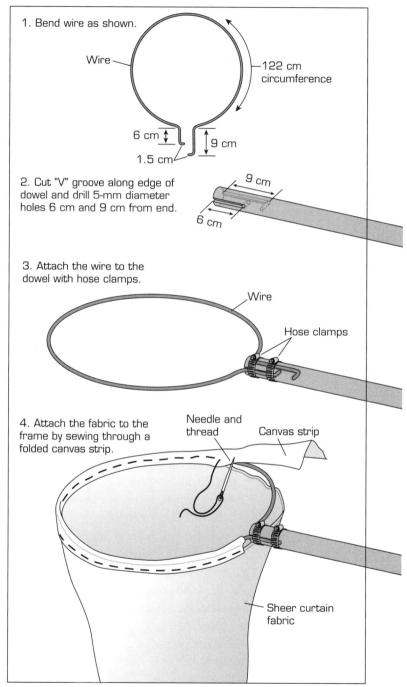

1. Bend wire as shown.

Wire

122 cm circumference

6 cm

9 cm

1.5 cm

2. Cut "V" groove along edge of dowel and drill 5-mm diameter holes 6 cm and 9 cm from end.

9 cm

6 cm

3. Attach the wire to the dowel with hose clamps.

Wire

Hose clamps

4. Attach the fabric to the frame by sewing through a folded canvas strip.

Needle and thread

Canvas strip

Sheer curtain fabric

Figure 22 Constructing a Butterfly Net

flower or leaf, quickly sweep the net sideways over it, then twist the handle a half turn. When you twist the handle, the netting will fall over the opening and prevent the insect from escaping. Gently grasp the body of the butterfly through the netting, just at the base of the wings, using your thumb and first finger. Holding a pair of blunt tweezers with your other hand, reach inside the net. With the tweezers, grab the butterfly firmly by the base of all four wings. You can now carefully withdraw the insect from the net and place it in a large, wide-mouthed jar for close observation with a hand lens. Be sure to release the butterfly near where you netted it.

Insect Holding Device

Keeping track of insect visitors to a flower can be a little tricky. One bee looks much like another! You can keep tabs of individuals by marking them with a small spot of nail polish or paint. A simple restraining device for small insects that sting or bite can be made from a large bore syringe 60 cubic centimeters (2 oz.), duct tape, a utility knife, and several 12-centimeter (5-in.) squares of plastic meshing cut from an onion or potato bag.

First remove the plunger from the syringe. Using a utility knife, cut off the tip of the syringe, so that the tube now has a straight, wide bore. ***Work carefully! The blades of these knives are very sharp.*** Cover the cut end of the syringe with two, overlapping squares of mesh material. Secure the mesh with duct tape.

Any bee or wasp that you mark must be anesthetized prior to placing it in the insect holder. Throw a few cotton balls soaked with ethyl acetate into the net after you have captured the insect. Once the insect has stopped moving, quickly drop it in the syringe, replace the plunger, and gently push until the insect is held firmly against the plastic meshing without crushing the insect.

Separate the meshing with forceps to open up a small window through which you can insert a toothpick or fine-tipped paintbrush. Be sure to record in your journal

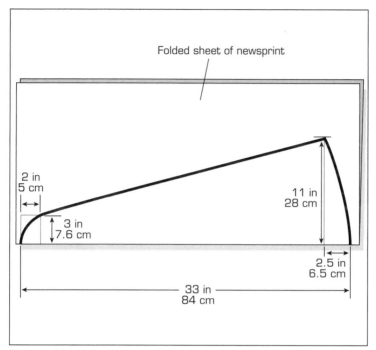

Folded sheet of newsprint

2 in
5 cm

11 in
28 cm

3 in
7.6 cm

2.5 in
6.5 cm

33 in
84 cm

Figure 23 Paper Pattern for Butterfly Net

the species and color and pattern of marking so that you can identify the creature when you spot it again. Work quickly and release the animal carefully!

Insect Rearing Cage

Insects, like caterpillars or grasshoppers, that you collect out on the prairie or even in the field behind your house can be successfully raised at home. An insect rearing cage can be constructed from an aquarium or small animal cage, a few plastic mesh strawberry containers, an ice pick or Philips screw driver, paper towels, and several plastic vials, jars, or drink cups with soft plastic caps.

Wash out the aquarium or animal cage thoroughly and dry it. Line the bottom with clean paper towels. Place two or three clean strawberry containers upside down and side by side in the cage. Fill a plastic container with water and cap it. With an ice pick or screwdriver, make a hole just large enough for the stem of plants that you will be feeding your captives. Set the capped container inside the cage, underneath the strawberry baskets. Introduce plant cuttings by poking the stems down through the mesh of the strawberry basket, then through the plastic container lid so that the plant stem is immersed in water. Place the lid on the cage and set it in a sunny room away from direct sunlight. Your insect cage is now ready for its first visitor!

To keep your insects happy and healthy, give them fresh, young leaves every day and be sure to change the paper towel liners. Remember, however, that these insects are wild creatures. Return them to their rightful environment after you are through observing them.

Killing Jar

If you want to make a permanent collection of the insects that you run across on your grassland excursions, you'll need a killing jar. To make one, collect a wide-mouthed pint or quart glass jar with a tight-fitting lid (mayonnaise jars work well), a clean plastic margarine or ice cream tub, plaster of Paris, permanent marker, masking tape, a spoon, measuring cup, scissors, blotting paper, and ethyl acetate. Ethyl acetate can be purchased from your pharmacist or a biological supply company (see Appendix). If you can't find ethyl acetate, substitute acetone or nail polish remover as the killing agent.

Mix up some plaster of Paris in a clean, disposable plastic tub using the directions provided by the manufacturer. Pour the wet mixture into a pint or quart glass jar, to a depth of $2\frac{1}{2}$ to 5 centimeters (1 to 2 in.). Let the plaster harden for 30 minutes. To thoroughly dry the plaster, place it in a warm oven (250°F or 121°C) overnight. Remove the jar the next morning and let it cool to room temperature.

Add killing agent (ethyl acetate or acetone) to the jar until the plaster is completely soaked and excess is beginning to pool. *Work in a well-ventilated place away from open flames or a heat source. Avoid breathing the fumes!* Pour off the excess liquid. Cap the jar tightly.

Cut a circle of blotting paper the size of the jar lid. Crumple up a second piece of blotting paper. Open the jar to place the paper circle on top of the plaster of Paris. Add the crumpled paper and close the jar. Wrap masking tape around the outside of the jar several times as a safety precaution in case of breakage. Label the jar "killing jar," list the killing agent, and date it.

To use the jar, place the insect inside and quickly screw on the cap. Within a few minutes, the insect will die relatively painlessly from the fumes of the killing agent. A quart-sized jar is suitable for larger insects including butterflies, while the pint container will work well for smaller insects. After several uses, add more killing agent to recharge the jar.

Because butterfly populations are declining and some species are now endangered, be very careful when collecting these fragile insects. Know the endangered or threatened species in your area. Keep them out of your net and out of your killing jar!

Plant Press

In your explorations of prairies and fields, you'll come across many beautiful wildflowers and interesting grasses. Try making a collection of a few of these. The best way to preserve the plants is to press them. Once dried, you can readily mount the specimens.

To make a press, you'll need a power saw, scissors, utility knife, a pencil, a meter stick, two sheets of 6-millimeter ($\frac{1}{4}$-in.) plywood each measuring 45 × 34 centimeters (18 × 12 in.), two $1\frac{1}{2}$-centimeter ($\frac{5}{8}$-in.) straps with metal buckles, 132-centimeter in length (52-in.), corrugated cardboard, blotting paper, and several old newspapers. The straps can be purchased from a camping or hiking supplier. Ask for discarded cardboard boxes at your local grocery store. Blotting paper, often used in desk pads, is sold at office supply stores or stationer's shops. You may substitute watercolor paper. You'll need enough cardboard to cut 10, 34 × 45-centimeter (12 × 18-in.) sheets and enough blotting paper to make 20 sheets of the same size.

With scissors or a utility knife, cut the blotting paper and corrugated cardboard to form a 34 × 45-centimeter (12 × 18-in) rectangle. *When using a utility knife, be very careful. The blade on this type of knife is razor sharp!* Use the scissors to trim 10 folded newspaper sheets to the same size as the cardboard and blotting paper.

Cut the plywood sheets to size with a power saw. *If you have never used this tool before, ask an adult to assist you.* Some home building suppliers or hardware stores may be able to do this work for you.

To assemble the press, place a cardboard sheet on top of a piece of plywood. Next lay two blotters followed by a cut sheet of folded newspaper. Add another two sheets of blotting paper. Top with a sheet of cardboard. Repeat the same arrangement of layers until you run out of cardboard pieces. When you've place the last cardboard sheet on the stack, top it with the second plywood piece. Loop a canvas strap around each end of the press.

To press a plant that you've collected, first remove any excess dirt or insects from the specimen. Open the press to expose a newspaper sheet. Now unfold the newspaper sheet. Arrange the plant specimen so that all plant parts are contained within the right half of the sheet (between the fold line and cut edges) and important features are illustrated. You'll probably have to fold the stems of some plants accordion-style to get them all on the sheet. Remember to include an identification number that corresponds to site and collection information recorded in your journal. Once you have the plant arranged, close the newspaper folder and replace the top half of the plant press. Tighten the straps to apply pressure. Place the press near a heat source or other warm spot to facilitate drying. After 24 hours, replace any newspaper sheets and blotters that appear damp or discolored.

Continue pressing the specimen. Replace the blotting

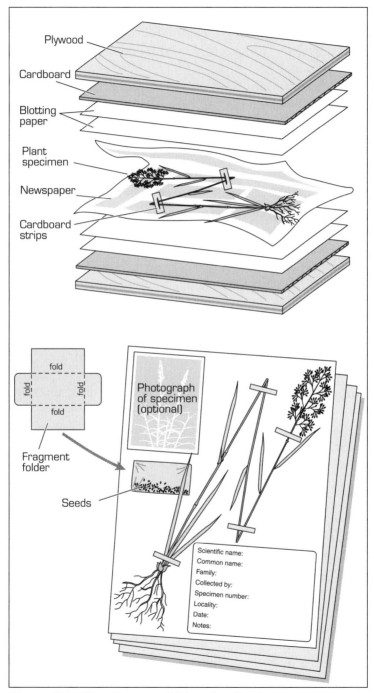

Figure 24 Plant Press and Mounting Card

papers and newspaper every 2 to 3 days for a 10-day period (blotting papers can be dried and reused). At the end of this period, the plants should be completely dry and ready to mount.

To mount the dried plant, make up a mixture of thinned white glue by adding one part of glue to two parts water (for example, add $\frac{1}{4}$ cup glue to $\frac{1}{2}$ cup water) and stirring. Sponge a thin layer of this mixture across the entire surface of the cookie sheet. Next, gingerly remove a dried plant from the plant press and place it on the coated cookie sheet. With your fingertips, press down all parts of the plant to thoroughly coat the back surface of the specimen. Now transfer the specimen to your mounting paper. Cover with a sheet of wax paper. Press to make sure that all parts of the plant make good contact with the paper. The glue should set within an hour. Remove the wax paper to let the mount dry completely.

Place a 7.6 × 12.7-centimeter (3 × 5-in.) index card in the lower right corner of the mounted specimen (preprinted labels can be purchased from scientific suppliers—see Appendix). Record the following information on each label: collector's name, specimen number, locality (give county and state at minimum), date collected, and habitat type. Leave room to record the scientific name, common name, and family name of the plant. Store mounted sheets in large boxes in a dry place.

Pooter

Some insects that you'll find on a prairie or field are too small to be easily captured by hand or with a net. The best way to catch these tiny creatures is with a pooter or aspirator. You can make one from a plastic jar with a lid (a peanut butter jar works well), airline aquarium tubing, a drill with $\frac{7}{32}$-inch drill bit, scissors, a small square of cheesecloth, a rubber band, hot glue and a glue gun, and a piece of scrap lumber.

Cut two pieces of aquarium tubing. Make the first piece 66 centimeters (26 in.) long and the second 25 cen-

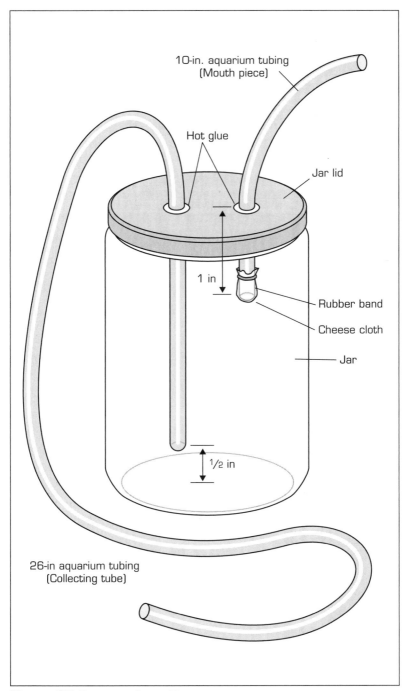

10-in. aquarium tubing
(Mouth piece)

Hot glue

Jar lid

1 in

Rubber band

Cheese cloth

Jar

1/2 in

26-in aquarium tubing
(Collecting tube)

Figure 25 Constructing a Pooter

timeters (10 in.) long. Next drill two holes in the jar lid using a $\frac{7}{32}$-inch drill bit. To prevent the lid from cracking, turn it upside down and back it with scrap lumber while drilling. Position the holes about 4 centimeters ($1\frac{1}{2}$ in.) apart.

Begin assembling the pooter by screwing the lid onto the jar. Slide the longest piece of tubing through one hole, until it's about 1 centimeter ($\frac{1}{2}$ in) from the bottom of the jar. Slide the shorter piece of tubing into the second hole so that only 2 to 3 centimeters (1 in.) protrude into the jar. Glue the pieces of tubing in place using hot glue and a hot glue gun. To seal the tubing on the undersurface of the lid, remove the jar lid.

The shorter piece of tubing serves as the mouthpiece; the longer piece functions as the collecting tube. By sucking through the mouthpiece when the jar is sealed, small insects can be pulled up into the jar through the longer piece of tubing. To prevent insects from being sucked into your mouth, wrap a small piece of cheesecloth around the end of the mouthpiece that's inside the collecting jar. Use a rubber band to hold the cheesecloth in place.

Sampling Frame

The best way to get to know a prairie is down on your hands and knees, one small patch at a time. Scientists often survey small plots or quadrats to get a feel for the plant species that live there and how they're arranged on the prairie. You can make a simple sampling frame using 200 centimeters (6 ft.) of $\frac{3}{4}$-inch polyvinyl chloride piping (PVC), a measuring tape, four $\frac{3}{4}$-inch 90-degree ell fittings, and a hacksaw. You can purchase these materials at most home building supply stores.

Use a hacksaw to cut four 50-centimeter (20-in.) pieces of PVC piping. Bring each PVC piece together using the ell fittings to form a square. The area contained within the square measures approximately $\frac{1}{4}$ square meter (2.7 square ft.)

To sample a plot, push the frame through the plants, all the way to the ground. Carefully pull out any stems or leaves that originate from outside the quadrant you are sampling. Now identify and record each plant growing within the PVC frame. Push aside the larger plants to look for mosses and other ground-hugging species.

Seed Cleaning Screen

Collecting seeds from a favorite wildflower or prairie grass is fun and easy to do. Once you've collected the seeds, you'll need to clean them by removing dried leaves and other plant parts. This protects the seeds from fungus and moisture. Most seed collectors use seed screens to process their seeds.

You can easily make your own with the following supplies: 200-centimeters (6-ft.) length of 1×4 pine or fir lumber (actual dimensions are $\frac{3}{4} \times 3\frac{1}{2}$ in.); 200 centimeters (6 to 8-ft.) of $\frac{3}{16} \times \frac{3}{4}$-inch wood trim; a sheet of aluminum or steel wire measuring 30×61 centimeters (12×24 in.), with a mesh size of 3 millimeters ($\frac{1}{8}$ in.); tin snips, small finishing nails; eight number 8 wood screws ($1\frac{1}{2}$ to 2-inch or 3.8 to 5.0-centimeter length); drill and $\frac{3}{32}$-inch drill bit; hot glue sticks and a hot glue gun; and a saw.

Cut the piece of lumber into four sections. Cut two 61-centimeter (24-in.) pieces and two 27-centimeter ($10\frac{1}{2}$-in.) pieces. Screw the pieces together with wood screws to form a box measuring 30×61 centimeters or 12 $\times$ 24 inches (see figure 26). Before placing the screws, drill pilot holes using a $\frac{3}{32}$-inch drill bit. Set the pilot holes back 2 centimeters ($\frac{3}{4}$ in.) from the long edge of the box.

With a pair of tin snips, cut the wire to form a $30 \times$ 61-centimeter (12×24-in.) rectangle. Anchor the sheet on top of the wood frame by running a bead of hot glue along the top of the frame. Quickly push the edges of the wire sheet into the glue and against the wood frame. *Be*

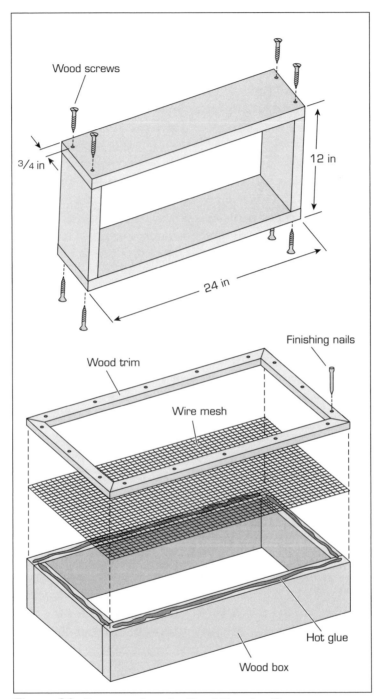

Wood screws

3/4 in

12 in

24 in

Finishing nails

Wood trim

Wire mesh

Hot glue

Wood box

Figure 26 Construction of a Seed Cleaning Screen

careful! The glue will be hot and could burn your fingers. Wear gloves or a use a pencil or stick to push the wire into the glue.

To finish the seed screen, cut the trim into four sections: two 30-centimeter (12-in.) pieces and two 27-centimeter ($10\frac{1}{2}$-in.) pieces. Nail the trim along the edges of the frame, on top of the screening. Position the finishing nails every 8 centimeters (3 in.) along the length of the trim, beginning 4 centimeters ($1\frac{1}{2}$ in.) from each corner.

Sweep Net

Many insects spend their entire lives hidden within the stems and blades of the grasses and wildflowers of a grassland. To capture them, scientists swing sturdy sweep nets through the grasses and forbs. This type of net can be made from the following materials: 61 centimeters (2 ft.) of $\frac{3}{4}$- or 1-inch wooden doweling; a strip of heavy canvas measuring 13 × 117 centimeters (5 × 46 in.); 150 centimeters of 9-gauge wire; 1 yard of a light-colored canvas or heavy cotton fabric; a sheet of newsprint or paper measuring 61 × 91 centimeters (24 × 36 in.); a meter or yard stick; two stainless-steel hose clamps ($\frac{9}{16}$ to $1\frac{1}{4}$-in.); a sewing machine or needle and thread; an iron and ironing board; scissors; straight pins; a measuring tape; a marker; a utility knife; pliers; a hammer; a screwdriver; a drill and $\frac{7}{32}$-inch drill bit. Purchase fabric from a fabric store and hose clamps from a hardware or auto-parts store. An old mop handle or broom handle can be used in place of the wooden dowel.

Follow the same basic steps as described for making a butterfly net: form the net, construct a pattern, cut out the fabric, sew the fabric, attach the net to the frame, and connect the net and handle. The figures on the next page provide the specifications for the sweep net, but use the instructions for the construction of the butterfly net given on the previous pages.

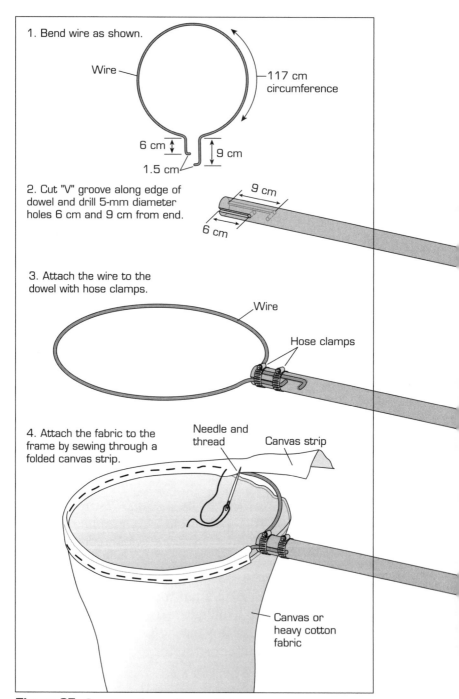

1. Bend wire as shown.

Wire

117 cm circumference

6 cm

9 cm

1.5 cm

2. Cut "V" groove along edge of dowel and drill 5-mm diameter holes 6 cm and 9 cm from end.

9 cm

6 cm

3. Attach the wire to the dowel with hose clamps.

Wire

Hose clamps

4. Attach the fabric to the frame by sewing through a folded canvas strip.

Needle and thread

Canvas strip

Canvas or heavy cotton fabric

Figure 27 Constructing a Sweep Net

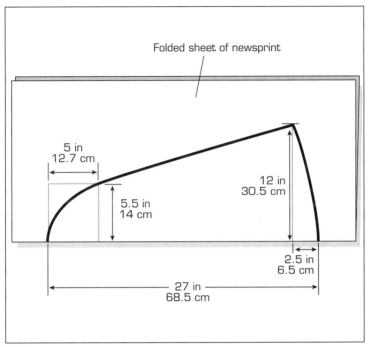

Folded sheet of newsprint

5 in
12.7 cm

12 in
30.5 cm

5.5 in
14 cm

2.5 in
6.5 cm

27 in
68.5 cm

Figure 28 Paper Pattern for Sweep Net

Three-Tiered Vertical Holder

You can learn a great deal about a grassland just by using your senses. Sometimes, however, prairie plants and animals are better at sensing their environment than we are. To feel what they feel or see what they see, scientists use special equipment and devices. To find out what temperatures a grasshopper, for example, experiences as it hops from the ground to a grass blade and then to its seed head, may require only something as simple as several thermometers and something to hold them in place.

A tiered vertical holder can be useful for monitoring environmental conditions from the ground up. To construct one, you'll need a 10-foot (3-meter) length of polyvinylchloride (PVC) piping that is 2 centimeters ($\frac{3}{4}$ in.) in diameter, a permanent marker, a ruler, a 7.5-m (25-ft.) tape measure, a hammer, three cardboard tubes

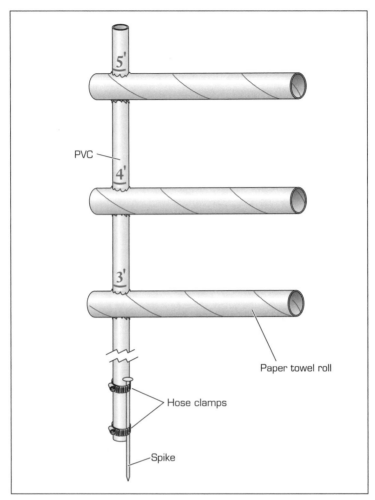

Figure 29 Three-tiered Vertical Holder

from paper towel rolls, a utility knife, three matched laboratory thermometers, one gutter nail at least 20 centimeters (8 in.) long, a screwdriver, two stainless-steel hose clamps ($\frac{9}{16}$ to $1\frac{1}{4}$-in.), and a saw.

Borrow several laboratory thermometers from your school science department. Use only those that read the same temperature when exposed to the same degree of heat or cold. Check them out by setting thermometers on an indoor table for 15 minutes. Read all thermometers at the end of this time and record temperature values in

°C or °F. Now place the thermometers in a rack in your refrigerator. Leave them for 15 minutes. Quickly remove and record the temperatures. Don't use any thermometer that is more than 2 degrees outside the group's average.

Cut 61 centimeters (2 ft.) off the end of the PVC piping and set it aside. Attach a gutter nail to one end of the long PVC pole using two hose clamps (see figure 29). The nail will help hold the pole upright in the ground. Lay at least 7 centimeters (3 in.) of the top part of the nail against the bottom 7 centimeters (3 in.) of the PVC pipe. The pointed end of the nail should protrude from the bottom of the pole. Slide two hose clamps over the nail and wood pole to hold the nail in place. Use a screwdriver to tighten the hose clamps until the nail is secure.

Mark heights on the PVC pole using a permanent marker. Beginning at the bottom (remember that the nail will be in the ground), mark the pole at 0.5-meter (or 1-ft.) increments. Record the height in meters or feet next to each marking.

Next prepare the cardboard tubes. Their job is to hold the thermometers vertically at different heights above the ground (see figure 29). As you look through one end a tube, hold the edge of a ruler across the opening so that it intersects the center of the circle formed by the end of the tube. Mark the points at which the ruler touches the top and bottom of the cardboard circle. Now lay the tube on its side. Mark an "X" 5 centimeters (2 in.) in from the end that you were looking through, just even with the first mark you made. Roll the tube 180 degrees. Measure a point 5 centimeters (2 in.) in from the same end, even with the second marking, with an "X." Using the utility knife, carefully cut through each X. *Watch your fingers as you work with the utility knife!* Enlarge the cuts by poking a finger through each X. Slide the pole through the cuts in the cardboard. The tube should be level and easily move up and down the pole. Prepare the remaining tubes in the same manner. Slide each on the pole and position them at the desired heights.

Glossary

allelochemical—a chemical produced and released by a plant to inhibit the growth of neighboring plants

anther—the pollen-bearing portion of a stamen

awn—a stiff bristle found on the scales of grass flowers

bison—an animal resembling an ox or cow, with a large head, shaggy mane, and large forequarters; in North America, commonly called a buffalo

blade—the broadest part of a leaf

bran—the broken seed coats of a cereal grain

calyx—the outermost ring or whorl of flower parts, usually consisting of small, green leaves called sepals

corolla—the ring of colored flower parts just inside the calyx, made up of several petals

disk flower—a specialized tubular flower found in plants of the daisy family

ecosystem—a distinct, self-supporting unit of interacting living forms and their environment

embryo—in plants, a minute plant bundled inside a hard, outer coat and supplied with food to be used during a period of rapid growth (germination)

endosperm—a tissue of seed plants that contains stored food for the developing plant embryo

floret—a specialized flower found in grasses, whose parts include a inner and outer scale usually enclosing pistils and stamens

forb—a nonwoody, flowering plant that is not a member of the grass family

glume—an empty scale found at the base of a cluster of flowers in a grass

gradient—a directional change in the value of a quantity along a two-dimensional axis

herbaceous—having little or no woody tissue, usually surviving only one growing season; if long-lived, persisting underground through the winter months

incubate—to place a specimen or sample under conditions optimal for growth and development

ligule—a minute outgrowth found at the junction of a grass sheath and blade, useful in the identification of grass species

mixed prairie—a region within North America's central grassland that exhibits grasses of medium height, sometimes also referred to as the midgrass prairie, mixed-grass prairie, or bluestem bunchgrass prairie

nectary—in flowering plants, a structure that secretes nectar, a sugary fluid that attracts animals to the plants

nematode—a group of animals possessing an elongated, cylindrical body, living free in the soil or in water, or living as parasites of plants or animals

nitrogen-fixing bacteria—a group of soil bacteria that can convert atmospheric nitrogen gas into chemicals useful to plants and animals; a common genus is *Rhizobium.*

node—the part of the stem to which the leaves attach

ovary—in plants, the enlarged, basal portion of the female part of a flower

over-wintering—in insects, to survive through the winter

ovule—a structure in seed plants that contains the egg cell and additional tissue

parallel—two lines, that when extended, never meet

perpendicular—two lines that meet at a right or 90° angle

petal—a highly modified, usually colored, leaflike structure found in flowers

pH—a measure of the relative acidity of a substance. It is rated on a scale of 1 to 14, where 1 is most acidic and 14 is least acidic

pistil—the female portion of a flower, consisting of an ovary, style, and stigma

pollen—a fine, powdery substance produced in the anthers of a flower, usually yellow or gold, containing the male sperm cell

pollinate—to transfer pollen from an anther to the stigma; can be accomplished by wind or animals

protozoan—a minute organism found in marine and freshwater habitats as well as moist terrestrial environments

pupate—the process of transforming from a larvae (such as a caterpillar) to an adult

rain shadow—the drier area on the lee side of a mountain

ray flower—a type of specialized flower found in plants of the daisy family, usually located on the periphery of the flower cluster

rhizome—a horizontal stem growing partly or completely underground, producing shoots and roots at the nodes

root nodule—a swelling or enlargement found on the roots of plants of the pea family (also called legumes), that are inhabited by symbiotic nitrogen-fixing bacteria

rush—a grasslike plant belonging to the family Juncaceae, exhibiting flowers very different from those of a true grass

sedge—a grasslike plant belonging to the plant family Cyperaceae, possessing triangular, solid stems unlike a true grass

sepal—the outermost flower whorl enclosing the petals and inner flower parts, usually consisting of small, leaf-like, usually green, bracts

sheath—that portion of a grass leaf that envelopes the stem

shortgrass prairie—the driest region of North America's central grassland, also known as the High Plains or Great Plains

sod—a thick mat of soil held together by the fibrous roots and underground stems of certain grasses

spikelet—a cluster of grass flowers made up of two empty scales or glumes at the base and two or more florets above

stamen—the male reproductive unit in a flower, usually composed of an anther and filament

stigma—the expanded tip of the style that receives the pollen grains

stolon—a runner; a trailing, above-ground shoot rooting at the nodes

stoma (pl. **stomata**)—a minute opening in the upper or lower cell layers of a leaf, through which water vapor, carbon dioxide, and oxygen pass

style—the stalk-like portion of a pistil that connects the ovary and the stigma

symbiosis—a close, physical, mutually beneficial association between two individuals of different species, in which both benefit

tallgrass prairie—the easternmost region of North America's central grassland, also known as the true prairie; a prairie where tall grasses reach heights of over a meter by mid to late summer

transect—in mapping, a line that runs from a baseline, along which distances to features of the landscape are measured

trichome—in plants, a hair-like outgrowth of the outer layer of tissue

For Further Information

Books

Brown, L. *Grasses, An Identification Guide*. Boston: Houghton Mifflin Company, 1979.

Brown, L. *Grasslands*. New York: Alfred A. Knopf, 1997.

Cushman, R.C. and S.R. Jones. *The Shortgrass Prairie*. Boulder, Colorado: Pruett Publishing Company, 1988.

Harrington, H.D. *How to Identify Grasses and Grasslike Plants*. Athens, Ohio: Swallow Press, 1977.

Ise, J. *Sod and Stubble. The Story of a Kansas Homestead*. Lincoln, Nebraska: University of Nebraska Press, 1936.

Ladd, D. *Tallgrass Prairie Wildflowers: A Field Guide*. Helena, MT: Falcon Publishing, Inc., 1995.

Madson, J. *Where the Sky Began. Land of the Tallgrass Prairie*. Ames, Iowa: Iowa State University Press, 1995.

Martin, A.C. *Weeds*. New York: Golden Press, 1987.

Milne, L. and M. Milne. *National Audubon Society Field Guide to North American Insects and Spiders*. New York: Alfred A. Knopf, 1995.

Mitchell, R.T. *Butterflies and Moths. A Guide to the More Common American Species*. New York: Golden Press, 1987.

Murie, O.J. *Animal Tracks*. 3rd ed., Boston, MA: Houghton Mifflin, 1985.

National Geographic Society. *Field Guide to the Birds of*

North America. 2nd ed. Washington, DC: National Geographic Society, 1987.

Pyle, R.M. *Handbook for Butterfly Watchers.* Boston, MA: Houghton Mifflin Company, 1992.

Stokes, D., L. Stokes, and E. Williams. *Stokes Butterfly Book. The Complete Guide to Butterfly Gardening, Identification, and Behavior.* Boston, MA: Little, Brown and Company, 1991.

Stubbendieck, J., S.L. Hatch, and C.H. Butterfield. *North American Range Plants.* 5th ed., Lincoln, Nebraska: University of Nebraska Press, 1997.

Whitaker, J.O., Jr. *National Audubon Society Field Guide to North American Mammals.* New York: Alfred A. Knopf, 1998.

Wilder, L.I. *Little House on the Prairie.* New York: HarperCollins Publishers, 1935.

Wilson, J. *Landscaping with Wildflowers. An Environmental Approach to Gardening.* Boston, MA: Houghton Mifflin Company, 1992.

Worster, D. *Dust Bowl. The Southern Plains in the 1930s.* New York: Oxford University Press, 1979.

Zim, H.S. and A.C. Martin. *Flowers. A Guide to Familiar American Wildflowers.* New York: Golden Press, 1987.

Videos

Tallgrass Prairie: An American Story. Washington, DC: National Geographic Society, 1997.

Organizations and Online Sites

Illinois Prairie Plants, Illinois Natural History Survey, *http://www.inhs.uiuc.edu/ ~ kenr/prairieplants.*

Kansas Prairie Wildflowers
http://spuds.agron.ksu.edu.wildflw.htm.

Konza Prairie
Division of Biology
Kansas State University
232 Ackert Hall
Manhattan, KS 66506
http://www.ksu.edu/konza

Meadowbrook Prairie
http://www.prairienet.org/meadowbrook.

Missouri Prairie Foundation
P. O. Box 200
Columbia, MO 65205
http://www.moprairie.org.

Monarch Watch
Department of Entomology
Haworth Hall
University of Kansas
Lawrence, KS 66045
http://www.MonarchWatch.org

National Wildflower Research Center
2600 FM 973 North
Austin, TX 78725

The Nature Conservancy
1815 North Lynn St.
Arlington, VA 22209
http://www.tnc.org

Northern Prairie Wildlife Research Center Web Site:
http://www.npwrc.usgs.gov/.

Equipment and Plant Suppliers

Abundant Life Seed Foundation
P.O. Box 772
Port Townsend, WA 98368
This nonprofit organization sells seeds for a number of plants, books, and seed cleaning screens.

Carolina Biological Supply Company
2700 York Rd.
Burlington, NC 27215
This company carries a wide variety of scientific equipment and supplies as well as living and preserved specimens. You can purchase insect nets, killing jars, plant presses, and herbarium paper from them.

Forestry Suppliers, Inc.
P.O. Box 8397
Jackson, MS 39284
One of the major suppliers for forestry and environmental needs. Offers insect nets and plant presses.

Prairie Moon Nursery
Rt. 3, Box 163
Winona, MN 55987
In addition to selling prairie plants and seeds, this nursery sells inoculant for use with legumes.

Prairie Nursery
P.O. Box 306
Westfield, WI 53964
http://www.prairienursery.com
One of the largest and best known prairie nurseries in the upper Midwest. Offers a full color catalog for a small fee. Well worth the money!

Index